OECD Compendium of Productivity Indicators 2016

OECD
BETTER POLICIES FOR BETTER LIVES

Please cite this publication as:
OECD (2016), *OECD Compendium of Productivity Indicators 2016*, OECD Publishing, Paris.
http://dx.doi.org/10.1787/pdtvy-2016-en

ISBN: 978-9264-25018-5 (print)
ISBN: 978-92-64-25019-2 (pdf)

Series: OECD Compendium of Productivity Indicators
ISSN 2225-2118 (print)
ISSN 2225-2126 (online)

Photo credits: Cover © Shutterstock/AnatolyM.

Corrigenda to OECD publications may be found on line at: *www.oecd.org/about/publishing/corrigenda.htm*.

Foreword

The OECD Compendium of Productivity Indicators *presents a broad overview of recent and longer term trends in productivity levels and growth across OECD countries and key partner economies. It highlights the key measurement issues faced when compiling cross-country comparable productivity indicators and describes the caveats needed in analyses. It examines the role of productivity as the main driver of economic growth and convergence, and the contributions of labour, capital and multifactor productivity to economic growth. It looks at the contribution of individual industries or sectors as well as the role of firm size and business dynamics. It explores the link between productivity, trade and international competitiveness, and analyses trends as compared with cyclical patterns in labour and multifactor productivity growth.*

The 2016 OECD Compendium of Productivity Indicators *was prepared in the OECD Statistics Directorate by Frédéric Parrot and Maria Belen Zinni, and edited by Nadim Ahmad and Mariarosa Lunati. The contributions of Liliana Suchodolska (Statistics Directorate) and Agnès Cimper (Directorate for Science, Technology and Innovation) are gratefully acknowledged.*

Table of contents

Tables

Figures

Follow OECD Publications on:

http://twitter.com/OECD_Pubs

http://www.facebook.com/OECDPublications

http://www.linkedin.com/groups/OECD-Publications-4645871

http://www.youtube.com/oecdilibrary

http://www.oecd.org/oecddirect/

This book has...

StatLinks

A service that delivers Excel® files from the printed page!

Look for the *StatLinks* at the bottom of the tables or graphs in this book. To download the matching Excel® spreadsheet, just type the link into your Internet browser, starting with the *http://dx.doi.org* prefix, or click on the link from the e-book edition.

OECD Compendium of Productivity Indicators 2016

Executive summary

Productivity growth is a central driver of long-term economic growth and living standards. But in many advanced and emerging economies productivity growth has been slowing. Against a backdrop of slower rates of investment coupled with increases in income and wealth inequalities, concerns are emerging that this may reflect a structural, and not a cyclical, slowdown, and a new low productivity growth paradigm, with consequential impacts on well-being and inequalities. Promoting productivity growth and sharing productivity gains, through the exploitation and creation of new and emerging technologies, investment in human capital (to meet the needs of 21st century production), and by fostering innovation, in particular through young firms, is as important today as it has ever been, to create a virtuous circle that tackles both growth and inclusion gaps.

Measuring productivity is difficult. There are challenges in the measurement of the factors of production, labour and capital, as well as the output. However, while these challenges can have an impact on recorded estimates and also impair international comparability, a growing body of evidence suggests that measurement, or rather "mis-measurement", is not the underlying cause of slower productivity growth.

Key results presented in the Compendium are summarised below:

Longer term trends

- Productivity growth remains below pre-crisis rates in many countries but the evidence points to the fact that labour productivity growth began declining before the crisis; with rates trending down since early 2000s in Canada, the United Kingdom and the United States and even earlier, and since the 1970s, in France, Germany, Italy and Japan.
- Over the last fifteen years, cross-country differences in GDP per capita growth can be mainly attributed to differences in labour productivity growth, as labour utilisation has increased only marginally. But the picture has been more varied since the crisis, particularly in those countries hit hardest and where employment levels have not recovered, i.e. hours worked per capita have fallen.
- Most of the growth in labour productivity reflected growth in multifactor productivity (MFP) and capital input. The empirical evidence points to the recent slowdown in labour productivity being at least in part explained by its pro-cyclical pattern, particularly for MFP, but longer term trends point to productivity slowing well before the current cycle.
- Sluggish business dynamism may also be hampering post-crisis productivity growth, with start-up and churn rates showing limited recovery in many countries.
- In general, productivity growth in manufacturing continues to outpace services. Within the business services sector, the key specialised services activity driving productivity

growth varied by country, for example, with professional services driving growth in Israel and information and communication services driving growth in Ireland.

- In most countries, labour productivity gaps between micro and, to a lower extent, SMEs and large firms, remain relatively high. This is particularly true for micro firms in both manufacturing and services.
- Increasing participation in global value chains is strongly associated with productivity growth in many, particularly Central Eastern European, countries. But the nature of participation and mode of upgrading varies across countries.
- Investment in knowledge-based capital (KBC) has been increasing over the past two decades, often at a faster pace than investment in traditional physical capital. KBC investment can contribute to foster economic growth and productivity and reinforce the contribution made by other production factors, through spillovers.

Recent developments

- In most OECD countries, labour productivity growth in the post-crisis period has been much weaker than in the pre-crisis period. While this decline has been broadly spread across sectors, labour productivity growth in the post-crisis period fell significantly in information and communication services, finance and insurance activities and professional services.
- In many emerging economies, post-crisis labour productivity growth has been much slower than in the pre-crisis period, partly reflecting their transition from industrial to services-based economies and the rebalancing towards consumption relative to investment.
- Similarly, there was a sharp fall in MFP growth in some countries, and there are risks that this could herald declining longer term trends in labour productivity growth.
- The flow of capital services has also slowed in most countries, partly reflecting the sluggish recovery of investment, in particular in tangible assets. Although investment in intellectual property products has been more resilient to the crisis; this too has slowed compared with pre-crisis rates.
- The corollary of slowing productivity growth in most countries post crisis has been relatively subdued wage growth, as countries sought to maintain competitiveness. This was particularly true in countries hit hard by the crisis, where low unit labour costs (ULC) went hand in hand with significant falls in employment and output.
- In sectors less exposed to international competition, notably the services sector, unit labour costs in some countries outpaced manufacturing ULC. But because many of these services are used as upstream inputs to manufacturers, international competitiveness could be impaired.

Reader's guide

Productivity is commonly defined as a ratio between the volume of output and the volume of inputs. In other words, it measures how efficiently production inputs, such as labour and capital, are being used in an economy to produce a given level of output. Productivity is considered a key source of economic growth and competitiveness and, as such, internationally comparable indicators of productivity are central for assessing economic performance.

This *OECD Compendium of Productivity Indicators* presents a broad overview of recent and longer term trends in productivity in OECD countries, providing insights on:

- international comparisons of income per capita and the role of labour productivity;
- the role played by labour and capital inputs and multifactor productivity in driving economic growth;
- the contribution of individual industries or sectors to aggregate labour productivity growth;
- differences in productivity across enterprise size classes;
- the links between productivity and international competitiveness;
- long term trends in productivity growth in major advanced economies.

Measures of productivity

There are many different productivity measures. The key distinguishing factor reflects the policy focus, albeit data availability can also play an important role.

Labour productivity, measured as Gross Domestic Product (GDP) per hour worked, is one of the most widely used measures of productivity at country level. Productivity based on hours worked better captures the use of the labour input than productivity based on numbers of persons employed (head counts). Generally, the source for total hours worked is the *OECD National Accounts Statistics* (database), although other sources are necessarily used where data are lacking. Work continues at the national level to develop the necessary source data but despite the progress and ongoing efforts, for some countries, the measurement of hours worked still suffers from a number of statistical problems that can hinder international comparability.

To take account of the role of the ***capital input*** in the production process, the preferred measure is the flow of productive services that can be drawn from the cumulative stock of past investments, such as machinery and equipment. These capital services are estimated by the OECD using the rate of change of the productive capital stock, which takes into account wear and tear, retirements and other sources of reduction in the productive

The statistical data for Israel are supplied by and under the responsibility of the relevant Israeli authorities or third parties. The use of such data by the OECD is without prejudice to the status of the Golan Heights, East Jerusalem and Israeli settlements in the West Bank under the terms of international law.

capacity of fixed capital goods. The price of capital services per asset is measured as their rental price. In principle, the latter could be directly observed if markets existed for all capital services. In practice, however, rental prices have to be imputed for most assets, using the implicit rent that capital goods' owners "pay" to themselves: the user costs of capital. The user cost (or rental price) for capital services reflect the amount that the owner of a capital good would charge if he rented out the capital good under competitive conditions.

After computing the contributions of labour and capital inputs to output growth, so-called ***multifactor productivity*** can be derived. It measures, therefore, the residual growth that cannot be explained by changes in labour and capital inputs and represents the efficiency of the combined use of labour and capital in the production process. Multifactor productivity is often perceived as a pure measure of technical change, but, in practice, it should be interpreted in a broader sense that partly reflects the way capital and labour inputs are measured. Changes in multifactor productivity reflect also the effects of changes in management practices, brand names, organisational change, general knowledge, network effects, spillovers from one production factor to another, adjustment costs, economies of scale, the effects of imperfect competition and measurement errors.

Gains in productivity also influence the development of ***unit labour costs*** one of the most commonly used indicators to assess a country's international competitiveness. However, the ability of unit labour costs to inform policies targeting international competitiveness may be limited. This relates to the increasing need to take into account the growing international fragmentation of production, the effects of which on competitiveness may not be captured sufficiently by unit labour costs.

The OECD *Productivity Statistics*

The indicators presented in this publication are drawn from the *OECD Productivity Statistics* (database), which provides a consistent set of annual estimates of labour, capital and multifactor productivity growth, unit labour costs and many other related indicators as a tool to analyse the drivers of economic growth in OECD member countries and emerging economies. The database includes the following indicators:

- GDP per capita and labour productivity levels
- Growth in labour productivity
- Measures of labour input, such as total hours worked and total persons employed
- Measures of capital input, as an aggregate and by type of capital good
- Share of labour costs in the total cost of production
- Multifactor productivity growth
- Unit labour costs

Annex A presents the definition of each indicator and the computation method.

Country, time and industry coverage

Most countries covered in this publication have recently updated their national accounts on the basis of the System of National Accounts 2008 (2008 SNA), which recognised, amongst other changes, that expenditures on research and development be treated as investment (Annex D). The pace of meeting the new standard varies across countries, meaning that some care is needed in cross-country comparisons. For Chile,

China, Colombia, India, Japan, Turkey and the Russian Federation the indicators are in line with the System of National Accounts 1993 (1993 SNA). For all the other countries, the indicators presented are based on the 2008 SNA.

Major revisions in international standards always provide countries with an opportunity to introduce quality improvements to their national accounts, by including newly developed and/or enhanced data sources and by improving their methodologies more generally.

The *OECD Compendium of Productivity Indicators* includes data for the following countries depending on data availability. The figures in this publication use ISO codes for country names as listed below.

OECD member countries:		
AUS Australia	**HUN** Hungary	**POL** Poland
AUT Austria	**IRL** Ireland	**PRT** Portugal
BEL Belgium	**ISL** Iceland	**SVK** Slovak Republic
CAN Canada	**ISR** Israel	**SVN** Slovenia
CHL Chile	**ITA** Italy	**ESP** Spain
CZE Czech Republic	**JPN** Japan	**SWE** Sweden
DNK Denmark	**KOR** Korea	**CHE** Switzerland
EST Estonia	**LUX** Luxembourg	**TUR** Turkey
FIN Finland	**MEX** Mexico	**GBR** United Kingdom
FRA France	**NLD** Netherlands	**USA** United States
DEU Germany	**NOR** Norway	
GRC Greece	**NZL** New Zealand	
Partner economies:		
BRA Brazil	**IND** India	**LTU** Lithuania
CHN China (People's Republic of)	**IDN** Indonesia	**RUS** Russian Federation
COL Colombia	**LVA** Latvia	**ZAF** South Africa

This publication looks at longer term trends in productivity growth but also at productivity patterns before and after the crisis. To this end, indicators are typically presented for distinctive time periods: 1995-2014; 2001-14; 2001-07; and 2009-14. For each country, the average value in the different periods only takes into account the years for which data are available for the respective indicator and its components.

Throughout this publication, the sectoral breakdown follows the International Standard Industry Classification of all Economic Activities (ISIC). Indicators by industry are presented according to its latest version, ISIC Rev. 4, or the European equivalent, NACE Rev. 2 (Nomenclature statistique des activités économiques dans la Communauté européenne).

Data are provided for the total economy and for selected sectors in the "non-agricultural business sector, excluding real estate" (ISIC rev. 4-codes B-N excl. L). These include: B – Mining and quarrying; C – Manufacturing; D – Electricity, gas, steam and air conditioning supply; E – Water supply; sewerage, waste management and remediation activities; F – Construction; as well as G-N excluding L – Business sector services, excluding real estate.

Business sector services (ISIC Rev. 4 codes G-N, excl. L) include: G – Wholesale and retail trade; repair of motor vehicles and motorcycles; H – Transportation and storage; I – Accommodation and food service activities; J – Information and communication; K – Financial and insurance activities; M – Professional, scientific and technical activities;

N – Administrative and support service activities. Real estate activities (ISIC Rev. 4 code L) are excluded, as their value-added includes the imputation made for the dwelling services provided and consumed by home-owners.

The business sector also excludes activities that are often provided by non-market producers. This reflects the fact that non-market activities are often measured on a sum-of-costs approach in current prices, with an implicit imputation made for labour productivity growth (usually zero) for volume estimates, together with an assumption of zero net operating surplus. These activities comprise: O – Public administration and defence; compulsory social security; P – Education; Q – Human health and social work activities; R – Arts, entertainment and recreation; S – Other service activities; T – Activities of households as employers; undifferentiated goods- and services-producing activities of households for own use; U – Activities of extraterritorial organisations and bodies.

OECD Compendium of Productivity Indicators 2016

Chapter 1

Measuring productivity

Productivity growth has been slowing in advanced economies since the mid-1990s, and more recently also in emerging economies. This decline has occurred at a time of rapid technological change, increasing participation of firms and countries in global value chains, and rising education levels in the labour force, all of which are generally associated with higher productivity growth. These seemingly contradictory facts have raised interest in the "productivity paradox" and whether the productivity slowdown is a transitional phenomenon or a longer-term condition. This chapter presents relevant evidence and discusses different views and explanations about the observed productivity trends. It also describes emerging challenges in measuring productivity and the way forward.

Considerable attention has focused in recent years on the productivity slowdown observed across OECD economies, dating back as far as the mid-1990s and earlier in some cases. More recently the slowdown has begun to be commonly referred to as the *productivity paradox*: a reference to the fact that the current slowdown has occurred at a time of significant technological change.

The advent of new (typically) digital innovations, such as Big Data, was expected to have sparked off a new wave of productivity growth, similar to those seen in the past, e.g. as a result of electrification and the ICT wave in the 1990s. But this has not, at least, yet materialised, raising a number of still largely open questions, ranging from potential lagged effects of these new technologies, to structural versus cyclical factors, right through to measurement.

While the jury remains out on the underlying causes, a growing body of evidence suggests that measurement, or rather "mis-measurement", is not the cause, or at least not the major cause (Syverson, 2016; Byrne, Fernald and Reinsdorf, 2016). This chapter brings together much of the evidence presented in this Compendium to provide, as far as possible, a single narrative on the slowdown story, while also taking the opportunity to present additional insights on the role measurement may play, particularly with regards to the "paradox".

The productivity slowdown and paradox

Until the mid-1990s, labour productivity growth in many OECD countries was relatively high compared with the United States, partly reflecting convergence towards the international productivity frontier (Figure 1.1) with productivity levels rising and, in some cases, surpassing those of the United States (Figure 1.2).

However, in many countries, the catch-up process went into reverse in the following decade (mid-1990s to mid-2000s), as productivity growth in the United States accelerated on the back of ICT led gains, outpacing productivity growth elsewhere. More recently, in the last ten years, productivity growth has slowed significantly, including in the United States, almost flat-lining in some major economies, as the effects of the ICT revolution began to fade.

The productivity slowdown observed in recent years has occurred at a time of rapid technological change, increasing participation of firms and countries in global value chains, and rising education levels in the labour force, all of which are generally associated with higher productivity growth. These seemingly contradictory facts have revived the debate on whether the productivity slowdown is a transitional phenomenon or a longer-term condition and a constraint to economic growth (see Box 1.1).

The current slowdown is not a recent affair

As highlighted above, the slowdown in labour productivity growth is a common feature among advanced economies and not a recent phenomenon; indeed underlying long-term trends suggest that the slowdown was underway prior to the crisis (Figure 1.3).

Figure 1.1. **Growth in labour productivity in advanced economies since 1970**

GDP per hour worked, percentage change at annual rate

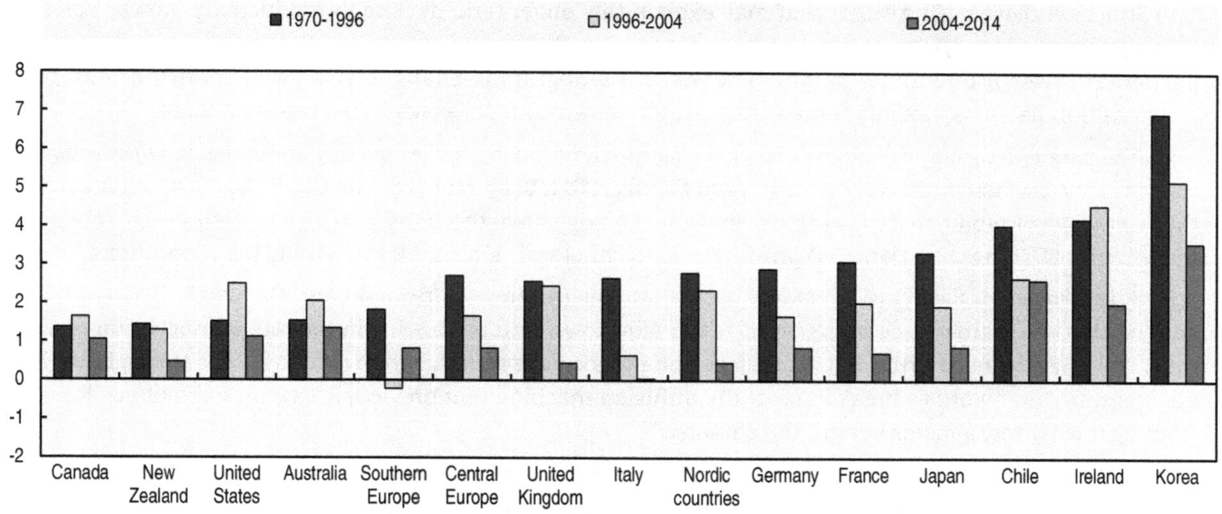

Note: Southern Europe includes Greece, Italy, Portugal and Spain; Central Europe includes: Austria, Belgium, Germany, Luxembourg, the Netherlands and Switzerland; Nordic countries includes: Denmark, Finland, Iceland, Norway and Sweden.

Source: OECD Productivity Statistics (database), *http://dx.doi.org/10.1787/pdtvy-data-en*, February 2016.

StatLink http://dx.doi.org/10.1787/888933346166

Figure 1.2. **Labour productivity levels in advanced economies**

GDP per hour worked, as percentage of the US, constant 2010 PPPs

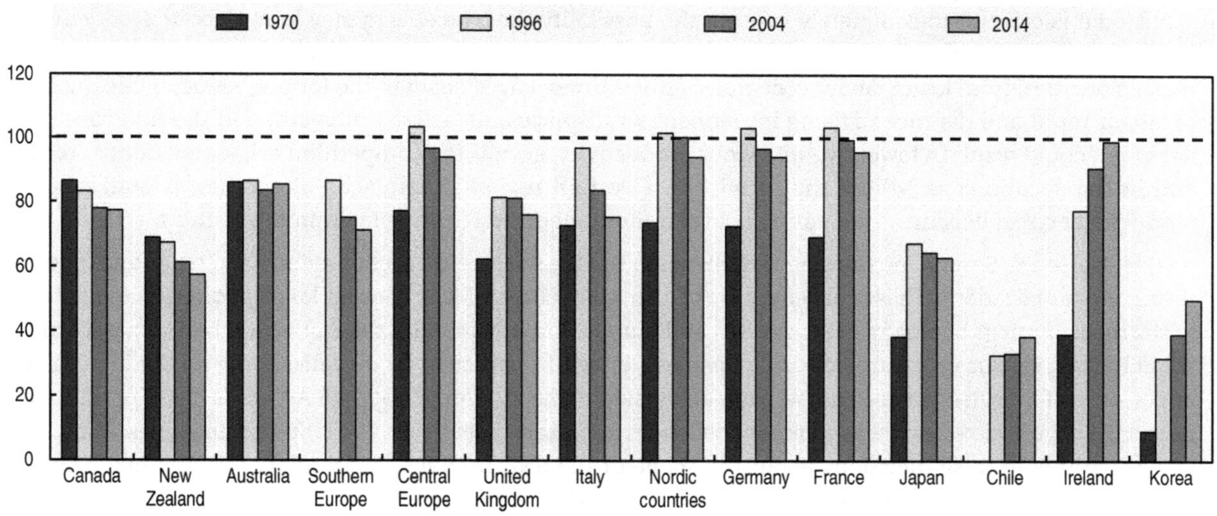

Source: OECD Productivity Statistics (database), *http://dx.doi.org/10.1787/pdtvy-data-en*, February 2016.

StatLink http://dx.doi.org/10.1787/888933346173

Box 1.1. **Explaining the paradox?**

A number of views have been put forward to address the apparent contradiction or paradox:

i) *The transformative nature and scale of today's technological breakthroughs pale into insignificance compared with those that took place in the last century* (electricity, internal combustion engines, medical breakthroughs, telephone and radio, which took years to fully spread out through the economy). Recent innovations such as ICT, although also revolutionary, saw more rapid adoption and have had a shorter-lived impact on productivity growth (Cowen, 2011; Gordon, 2012).

Box 1.1. **Explaining the paradox?** *(cont.)*

ii) *Structural changes.* One factor that may explain the longer term decline in productivity growth across, particularly developed, economies may be the long term shift from manufacturing to services, including in particular lower productivity personal services. Demographic changes and more service orientated consumption patterns, notably from ageing populations may have exacerbated these impacts.

iii) *The pace of technological progress has not slowed but adoption requires parallel innovation in organisational structures and business models* (Brynjolfsson and McAfee, 2011; Baily, Manyika and Gupta, 2013). In other words, the next wave of productivity growth driven by technology breakthroughs in artificial intelligence, robotics, the Internet of Things, Big Data, 3-D printing, nanotechnology, biotechnology, may lag the innovations.

iv) *A breakdown of the diffusion machine.* Some studies (Andrews, Criscuolo and Gal, 2015; OECD, 2015a) suggest that the main source of the productivity slowdown is not a slowing in the rate of innovation by the most globally advanced firms, but rather a slowing of the pace at which innovations spread throughout the economy. In other words a breakdown of the diffusion machine that previously saw productivity spill-over from frontier firms, a factor behind the paradox.

v) *Rent reducing transformation.* Another possibility is that many of the new technologies, in particular those related to the digital economy such as Big Data and e-commerce, may have a different transformative role than earlier technological innovations. These earlier innovations, including classic ICT innovations such as computers and software, often resulted in profound changes to the production process of goods and services. Many of today's new innovations, notably e-commerce and to a lesser extent some applications of Big Data, on the contrary, are less about transforming (i.e. introducing efficiencies in the production process) and more about expanding markets, where productivity gains are generated through improved economies of scale rather than transformative changes in the production process.

Indeed it is difficult to completely rule out the possibility that the effects may lower labour productivity (but not necessarily multifactor productivity), as competition in relatively high labour cost countries, regions or cities, from lower labour cost areas, either drives wages down in the former, reducing the quality of labour input and dis-incentivising investment, or displaces the activity altogether. In the first case the net effect could result in lower overall labour productivity, even if the competition originates from abroad; and in the second case, where the activity in a certain region is displaced altogether, overall labour productivity could decline at the national level if the competition is driven within the country.

vi) *Measurement.* Several measurement challenges limit the analysis of recent productivity trends and indeed their policy implications. These challenges are of course not all new. Many concern longstanding issues relating to the measurement of factors of production and output, and in particular the distinction between price and volume changes. But new forms of doing business, driven in particular by digitalisation, and the increasing importance of knowledge-based assets that are outside of the System of National Accounts (SNA) production boundary, have added new measurement challenges and exacerbated even the long standing ones. They are also beginning to raise questions about the scope of the SNA production boundary itself as households increasingly engage in activities that once would have been the preserve of intermediaries through the use of free services (e.g. search engines). These have been further complicated by the growing importance of global value chains in the production process. Increased specialisation in tasks within an industry in a given country may complicate simple analyses of value added, and so productivity, at the sectoral level that implicitly assume that a similar activity (or rather task) is being undertaken over comparable periods of time. The increasing importance of multinationals and indeed their ability to engage in profit shifting across affiliates, adds a further layer of complication, particularly for measures of multifactor productivity, as the potential for inconsistencies between where factors of production and output are recorded increases. The last section in this Chapter provides a more thorough assessment of measurement challenges.

One important thing to note from the above is that none of the potential causes is mutually exclusive. All or some could explain the paradox, and so they should be viewed as complementary.

Figure 1.3. **Trend labour productivity growth in G7 countries**

Total economy, percentage change at annual rate

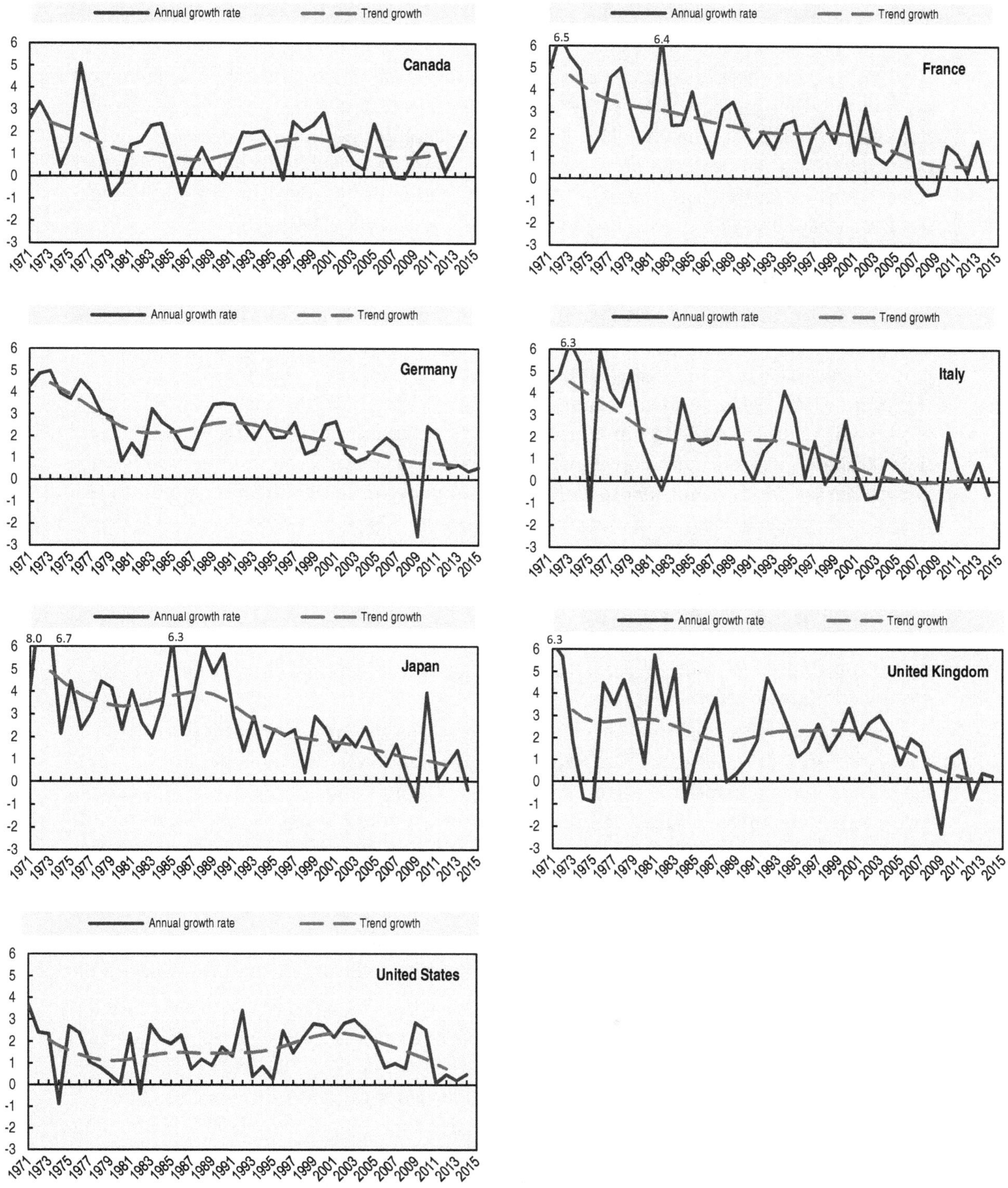

Source: OECD Productivity Statistics (database), *http://dx.doi.org/10.1787/pdtvy-data-en*, February 2016.

StatLink *http://dx.doi.org/10.1787/888933346189*

Declining trends in labour productivity growth are largely characterised by slower growth in multifactor productivity (MFP), lending some weight to the arguments that technological spillovers and diffusions from ICT, and other new technologies may be lower than from earlier technology breakthroughs.

The evidence here is not conclusive. For example, declining trends may, at least in part also reveal other inefficiencies in the combined utilisation of labour and capital inputs, notably from skills mismatches (Box 1.2) but also capital misallocation. Moreover, lower MFP growth has not been the only component driving down labour productivity, in many countries the contribution of capital deepening, particularly in recent years, reflecting weaker investment, has also begun to trend downwards (Figure 1.4).

And the contribution from investment in ICT has slowed significantly

The direct contribution of ICT capital goods to productivity reached its peak in the late 1990s and started to diminish in the early 2000s. Considerable improvements in the price-performance ratio of ICT capital (and Moore's law) saw significant take-up of ICT capital in the mid to late 1990s, with correspondingly significant contributions to overall labour productivity growth. Although investment in ICT remained relatively high at the turn of the 2000s and onwards, and continued to play an important role in driving productivity growth across OECD countries, these contributions began to decline almost across the board, with sizeable declines in many countries (Figure 1.5).

While the shares of ICT investment have held up reasonably well compared with other forms of investment, ICT investment as a share of GDP in recent years remains below previous highs, significantly so in some countries (Figure 1.6).

Although the slowing contribution from ICT may reflect increased investment in other knowledge-based assets

Investment in ICT capital also contributes indirectly to productivity growth, as it supports firms in innovating and improving organisational and managerial practices, including the management of sales, inventories, customers and supply chains. ICT capital investment thus often requires complementary investments in knowledge-based capital (KBC), such as patents, design, firm-specific training, organisational and managerial capabilities and the experimentation with new technologies in the form of research and development. Currently however, with the exception of software and research and development, most of the investment in KBC are outside of the System of National Accounts (SNA) production boundary, and so are not included in the investment and capital figures shown in the Compendium.

Recent studies show that investment in KBC has been increasing over the past two decades, often at a faster pace than investment in traditional physical capital (OECD, 2015b). In 2013, investment in all types of KBC amounted to around 1.5 times investment in fixed assets in the United States and the United Kingdom, 80% in France, 90% in Germany and just under half in Italy and Spain (Figure 1.7). That being said *The Future of Productivity (OECD, 2015)* pointed to a slowing in the pace of KBC investment that started prior to the crisis, which may have led to lower spillover effects for MFP.

But increased investment in other knowledge-based assets only adds to the paradox

The current exclusion of many knowledge-based assets from the SNA production boundary cannot automatically be used to explain the paradox however, as their exclusion

Figure 1.4. **Labour productivity growth, capital deepening and MFP in G7 countries**

Total economy, percentage change at annual rate

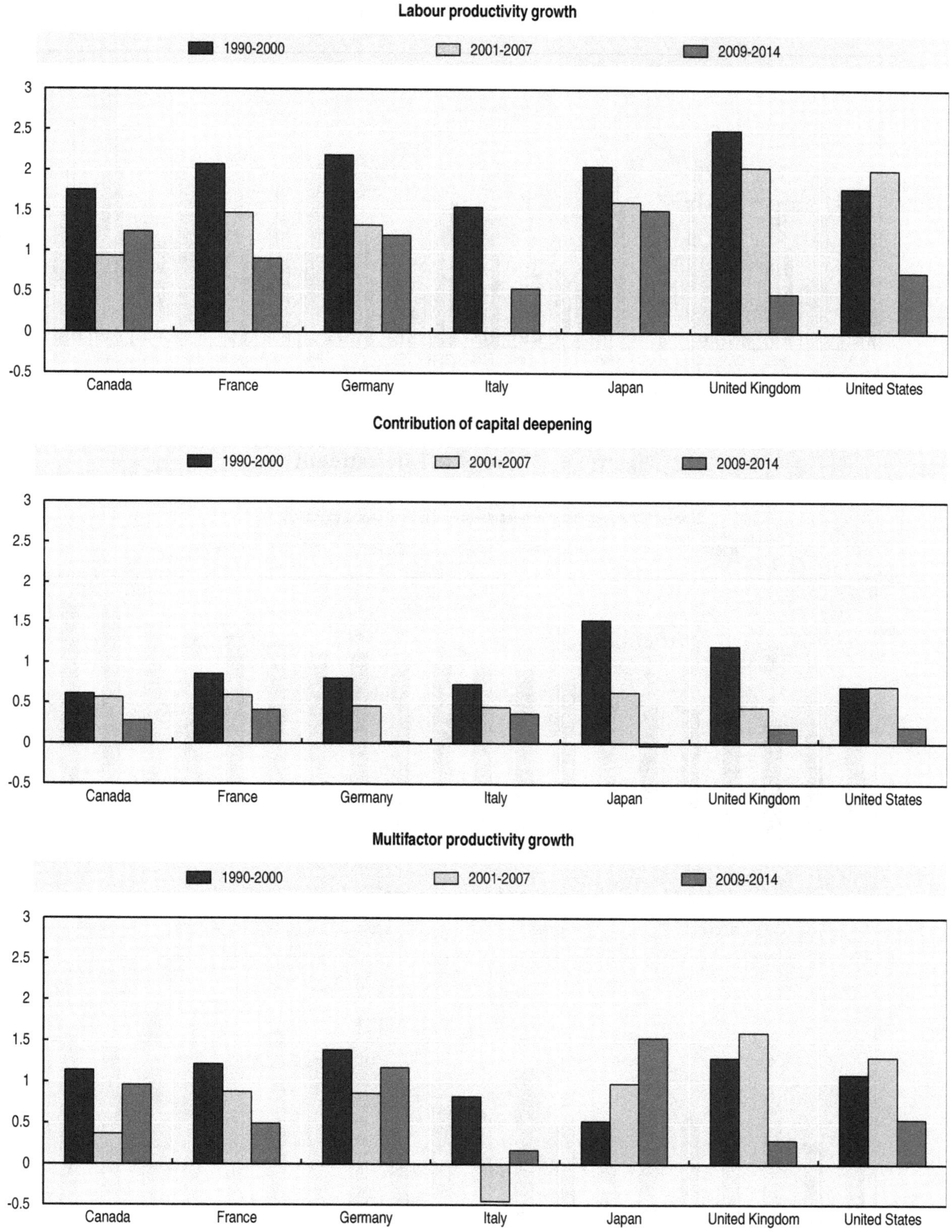

Source: OECD Productivity Statistics (database), *http://dx.doi.org/10.1787/pdtvy-data-en*, February 2016.

StatLink http://dx.doi.org/10.1787/888933346196

Figure 1.5. **Contribution of ICT capital deepening to labour productivity growth**

Percentage change at annual rate

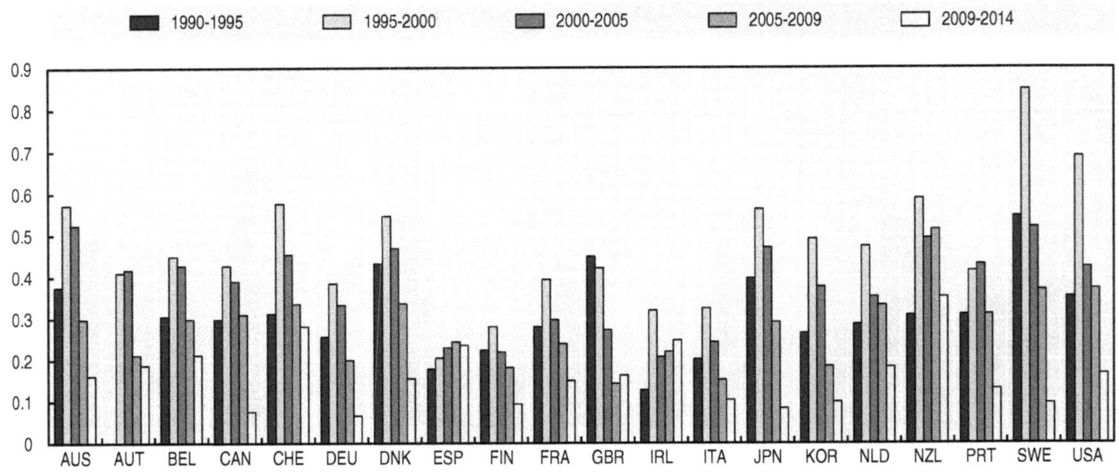

Source: OECD Productivity Statistics (database), *http://dx.doi.org/10.1787/pdtvy-data-en*, February 2016.

StatLink http://dx.doi.org/10.1787/888933346208

Figure 1.6. **Share of ICT investment**

Percentage of non-residential gross fixed capital formation and percentage of GDP

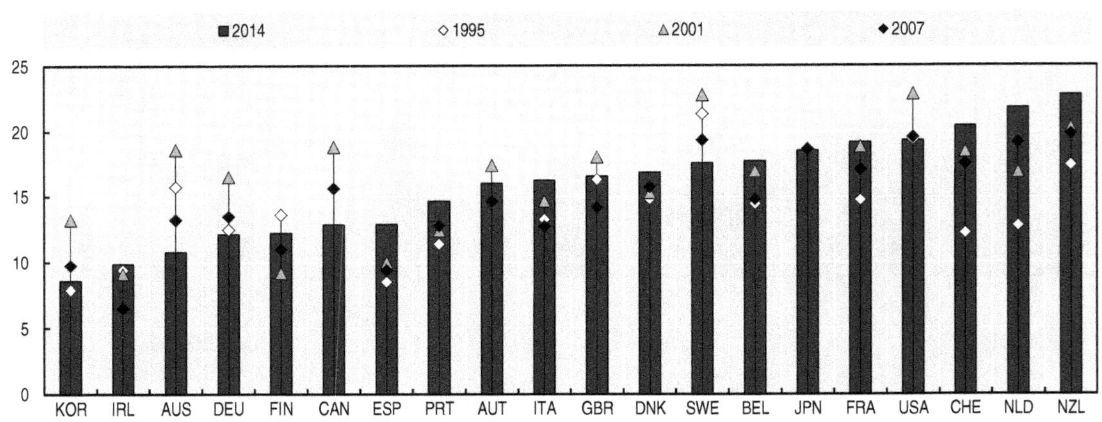

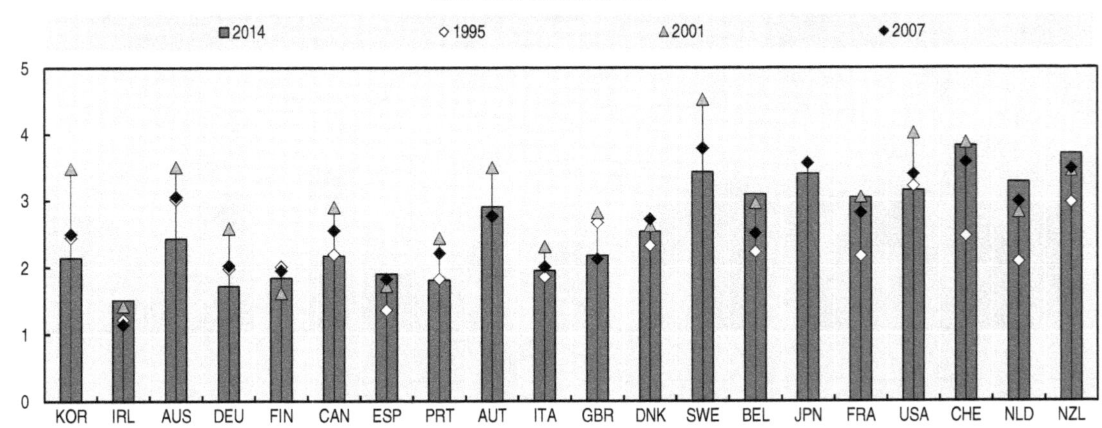

Source: OECD Productivity Statistics (database), *http://dx.doi.org/10.1787/pdtvy-data-en*, February 2016.

StatLink http://dx.doi.org/10.1787/888933346215

Figure 1.7. **Business investment in fixed and knowledge-based capital, selected economies, 2013**

As percentage of business sectors' gross value added

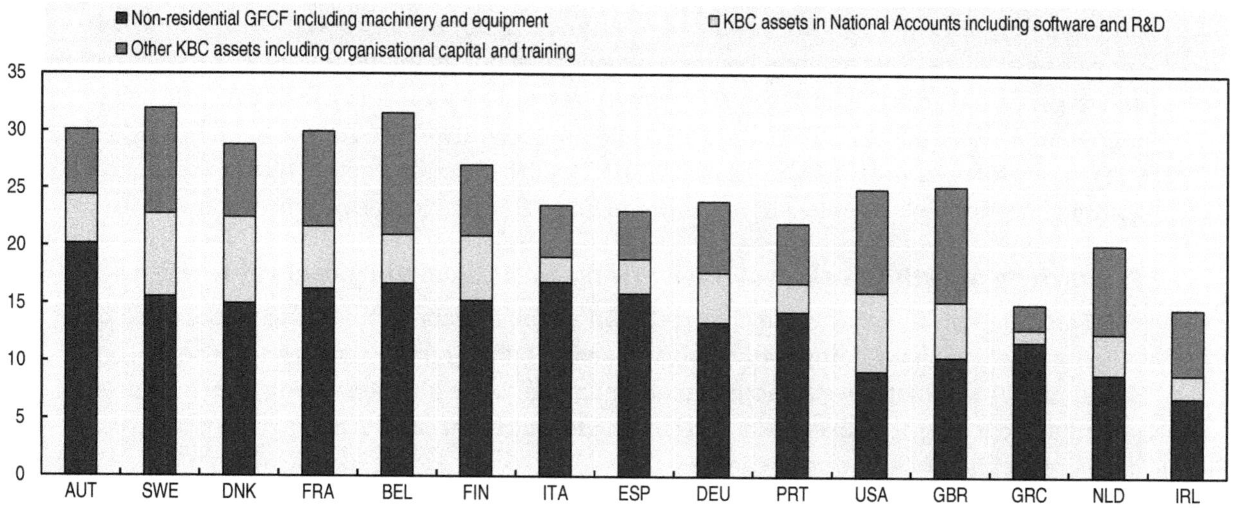

Source: OECD (2015b), OECD Science, Technology and Industry Scoreboard 2015: Innovation for growth and society, OECD Publishing, Paris, *http://dx.doi.org/10.1787/sti_scoreboard-2015-en*.

StatLink http://dx.doi.org/10.1787/888933346223

Box 1.2. **Productivity and skills mismatch**

While the specific knowledge of highly educated workers can directly increase business performance, a skilled workforce can also act indirectly on productivity via improved technologies, business models and organisational practices, reinforcing the benefits of investment in physical and knowledge-based capital (KBC).

However, according to the recent OECD Survey of Adult Skills (PIAAC), there are significant shares of workers in OECD countries that are over or under-qualified for their job, with high shares also reporting a mismatch between their existing skills and those required for their job (OECD, 2013). This implies that there is scope for improving the efficiency of human capital allocation in OECD countries, possibly affecting aggregate productivity.

The links between skills mismatch and labour productivity have been recently explored by OECD work, exploiting data from the PIAAC survey (Andrews and Adalet Mc Gowan, 2015). The existing body of literature already emphasised that under-qualification and under-skilling are associated with lower labour productivity within the affected firm. The important insight of the recent work is that skill and qualification mismatch is associated with lower aggregate labour productivity. In particular, the impact of over-skilling on productivity results from its effects on allocative efficiency: in industries with a higher share of over-skilled workers, more productive firms find it more difficult to attract suitable labour that could allow expanding their operations. The conclusion seems to indicate that the allocation of skills can potentially account for a relevant share of cross-country productivity gaps, complementing recent findings showing that the level of skills can explain 30%-40% of the cross-country variation in aggregate labour productivity (OECD, 2013).

Finally, there is a link between managerial quality and mismatch; a more efficient matching of qualifications and skills is one of the possible channels through which higher managerial quality increases productivity.

Source: Andrews and Adalet Mc Gowan, 2015; OECD, 2013.

means that their indirect impact is currently captured with estimates of MFP, and so the evidence pointing to rising shares of KBC merely serves to reinforce the paradox.

Recent analysis that explores the links between business investment in KBC and productivity performance (Andrews and Westmore, 2013; Andrews and Criscuolo, 2014) provides some possible insights. Preliminary evidence points to two findings: the speed of convergence towards the long-run MFP growth rates seems to be faster in countries with high managerial quality and business R&D and, importantly in the context of the paradox, the returns to investing in KBC appear to be affected by structural factors that influence the ability of economies to reallocate resources to firms that invest in this type of capital.

Productivity growth has slowed despite rising participation in global value chains

Participation in global value chains (GVCs) enables firms to specialise in activities or tasks where they have comparative advantages, providing opportunities to benefit from economies of scale as they gain access to new markets, while also benefitting from increased potential technology spillovers. Moreover, by increasing international competition, GVCs put pressure on firms to innovate to succeed.

Measured on the basis of the foreign content of gross exports, the evidence shows that integration in GVCs has increased significantly since the mid-1990s (Figure 1.8). The evidence also indicates a positive, but nuanced, relationship between participation in GVCs and productivity growth (Figure 1.9). While the overwhelming evidence supports the existence of strong positive relationships between GVC integration and growth, integration in GVCs requires indeed a holistic policy approach. In some countries, for example, the evidence points to getting locked in the middle-income trap, and in others, the reallocation of workers in tasks facing competition from lower labour cost countries may be suboptimal, with potential increases in skills mismatches.

Figure 1.8. **Foreign value added share of gross exports**

Percentage

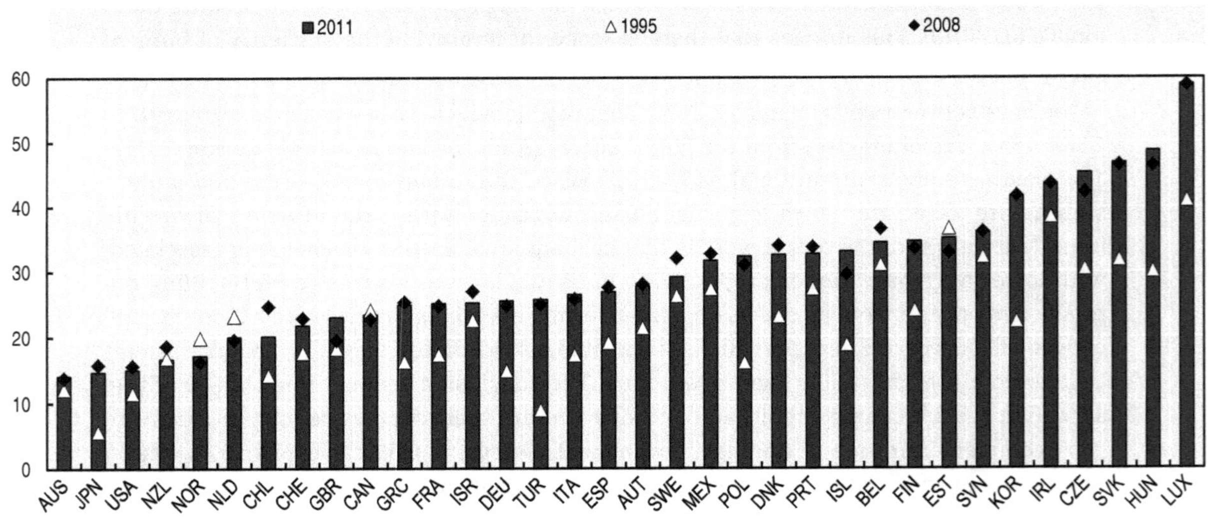

Source: OECD-WTO: Statistics on Trade in Value Added (database), *http://dx.doi.org/10.1787/data-00648-en*.

StatLink http://dx.doi.org/10.1787/888933346230

Figure 1.9. **Integration in GVCs and productivity**

Total economy

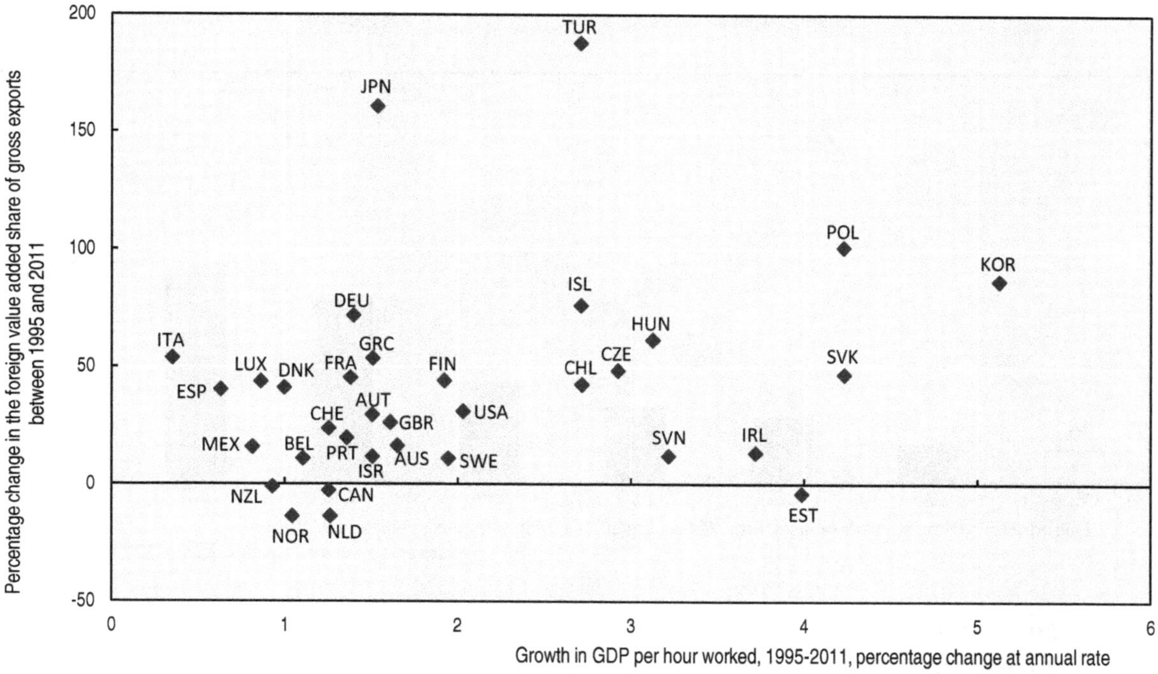

Source: OECD Productivity Statistics (database), *http://dx.doi.org/10.1787/pdtvy-data-en*, February 2016 and OECD-WTO: Statistics on Trade in Value Added (database), *http://dx.doi.org/10.1787/data-00648-en*.

StatLink http://dx.doi.org/10.1787/888933346240

And the slowdown is not confined to developed economies

The evidence supporting the relationship between higher integration in GVCs and higher productivity is particularly strong for developing economies but recently, the slowdown in labour productivity growth has also extended to emerging economies (Figures 1.10 and 1.11).

Figure 1.10. **Labour productivity levels in emerging economies**

GDP per person employed, as percentage of the US, constant 2010 PPPs

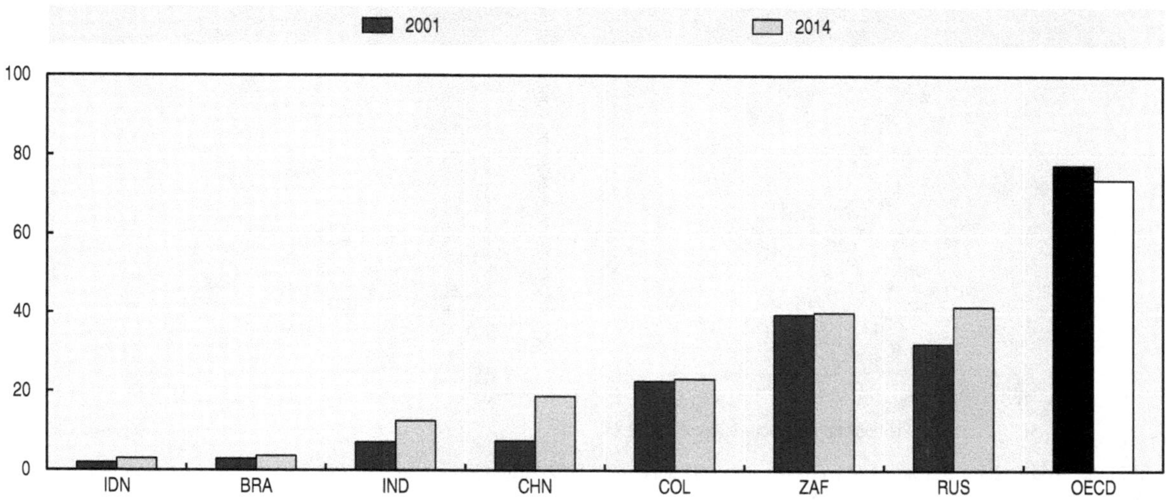

Source: OECD Productivity Statistics (database), *http://dx.doi.org/10.1787/pdtvy-data-en*, February 2016.

StatLink http://dx.doi.org/10.1787/888933346255

Figure 1.11. **Labour productivity growth in emerging economies**

GDP per person employed, percentage change at annual rate

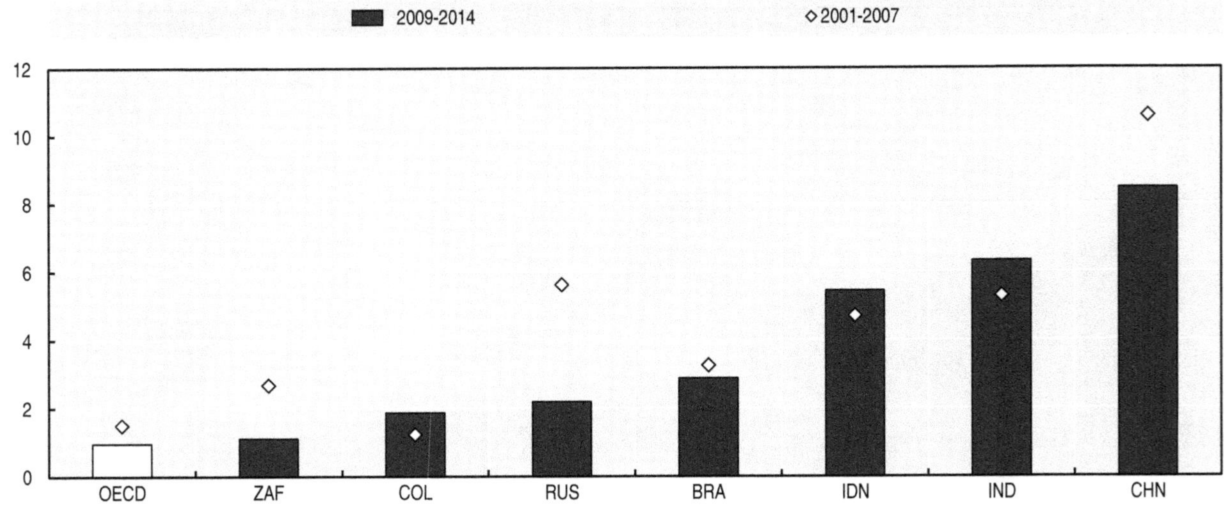

Source: OECD Productivity Statistics (database), *http://dx.doi.org/10.1787/pdtvy-data-en*, February 2016.

StatLink http://dx.doi.org/10.1787/888933346267

Sluggish business dynamism adds further concerns to productivity growth

In many countries the slowdown of productivity growth, has been coupled with sluggish business dynamism. The evidence shows a strong relationship between labour productivity growth and start-up rates and churn rates, i.e. the sum of birth and death rates (Figure 1.12). New firms contribute to the creation of novel ideas, and competition with incumbent firms stimulates the latter to introduce productivity-enhancing changes (e.g. improved managerial

Figure 1.12. **Labour productivity growth and business dynamism**

Share of employer firms with 0-2 years in total firm population (left) and churn rates (right) on x-axis and GDP per hour worked, percentage change at annual rate on y-axis

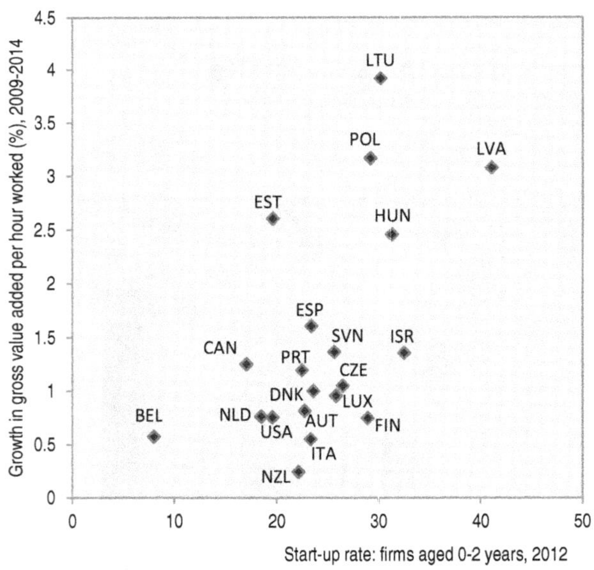

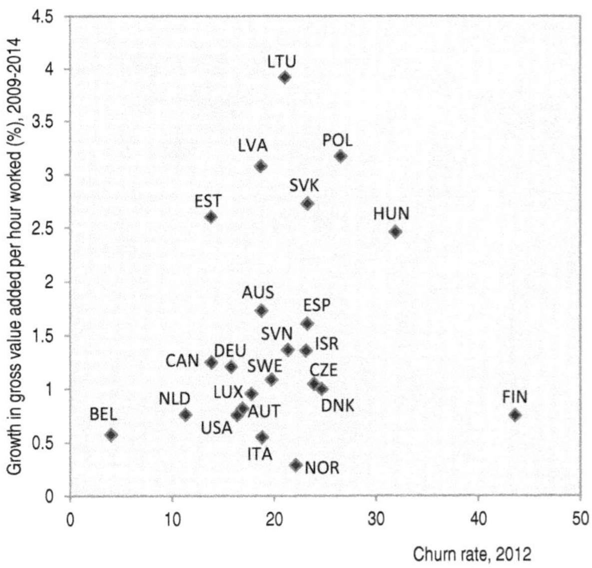

Source: OECD Productivity Statistics (database), *http://dx.doi.org/10.1787/pdtvy-data-en* and OECD Structural and Demographic Business Statistics (database), *http://dx.doi.org/10.1787/sdbs-data-en*.

StatLink http://dx.doi.org/10.1787/888933346270

practices, adoption of new technologies, etc.), thus contributing to increase aggregate productivity growth. Churn rates illustrate the creative destruction process, whereby new (innovative) firms enter and expand while displacing less productive firms. This reallocation of resources is expected to increase aggregate productivity.

In recent years, though, the start-up and churn rates have generally declined in OECD countries, with a few exceptions (Figures 1.13 and 1.14). Andrews, Bartelsman and Criscuolo (2015) show that for eight European countries MFP growth over the 2000s was weaker in sectors that recorded larger declines in the share of young firms (under six years), and in particular start-ups (under three years).

Figure 1.13. **Start-up rates, total business economy**

Share of employer firms with 0-2 years in total firm population, average of the period

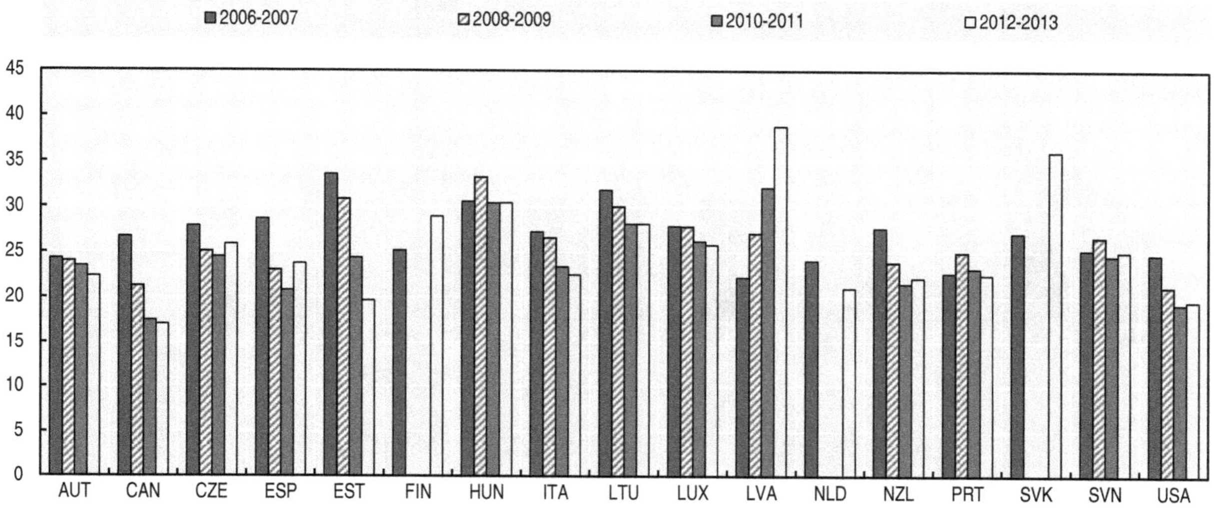

Source: OECD Structural and Demographic Business Statistics (database), *http://dx.doi.org/10.1787/sdbs-data-en.*

StatLink http://dx.doi.org/10.1787/888933346285

Figure 1.14. **Churn rates, employer enterprises, total business economy**

Percentage

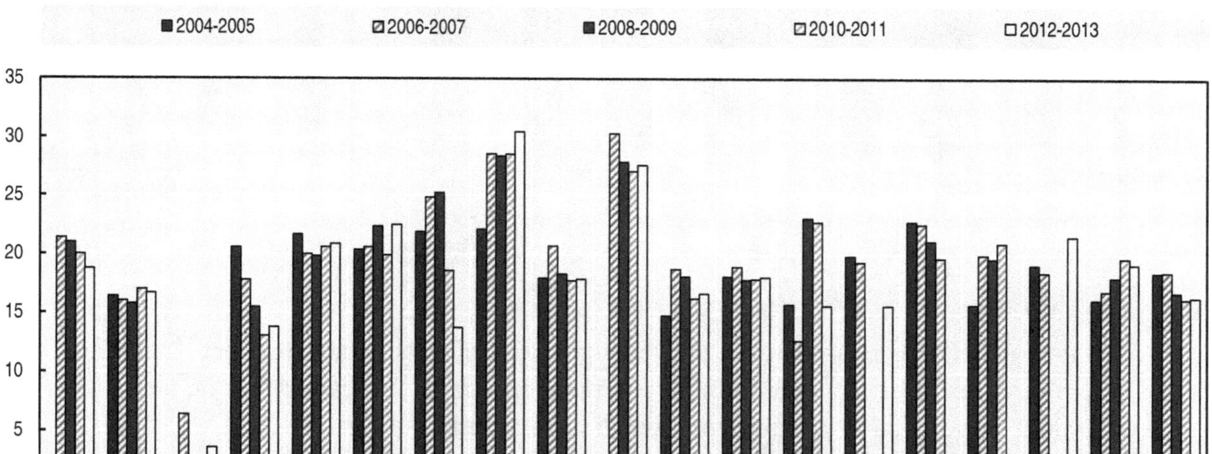

Source: OECD Structural and Demographic Business Statistics (database), *http://dx.doi.org/10.1787/sdbs-data-en.*

StatLink http://dx.doi.org/10.1787/888933346296

Firm heterogeneity also matters for productivity. To the extent that large firms can exploit increasing returns to scale, productivity typically increases with firm size. In fact, larger firms show almost consistently higher levels of productivity than micro and small enterprises (Figure 1.15). Interestingly, the gap in productivity between firms of different sizes increased in the manufacturing sector from 2008 to 2013, while not always in the services sector.

Figure 1.15. **Labour productivity by firm size**

Value added per person employed, large firms (250 workers or more) = 100

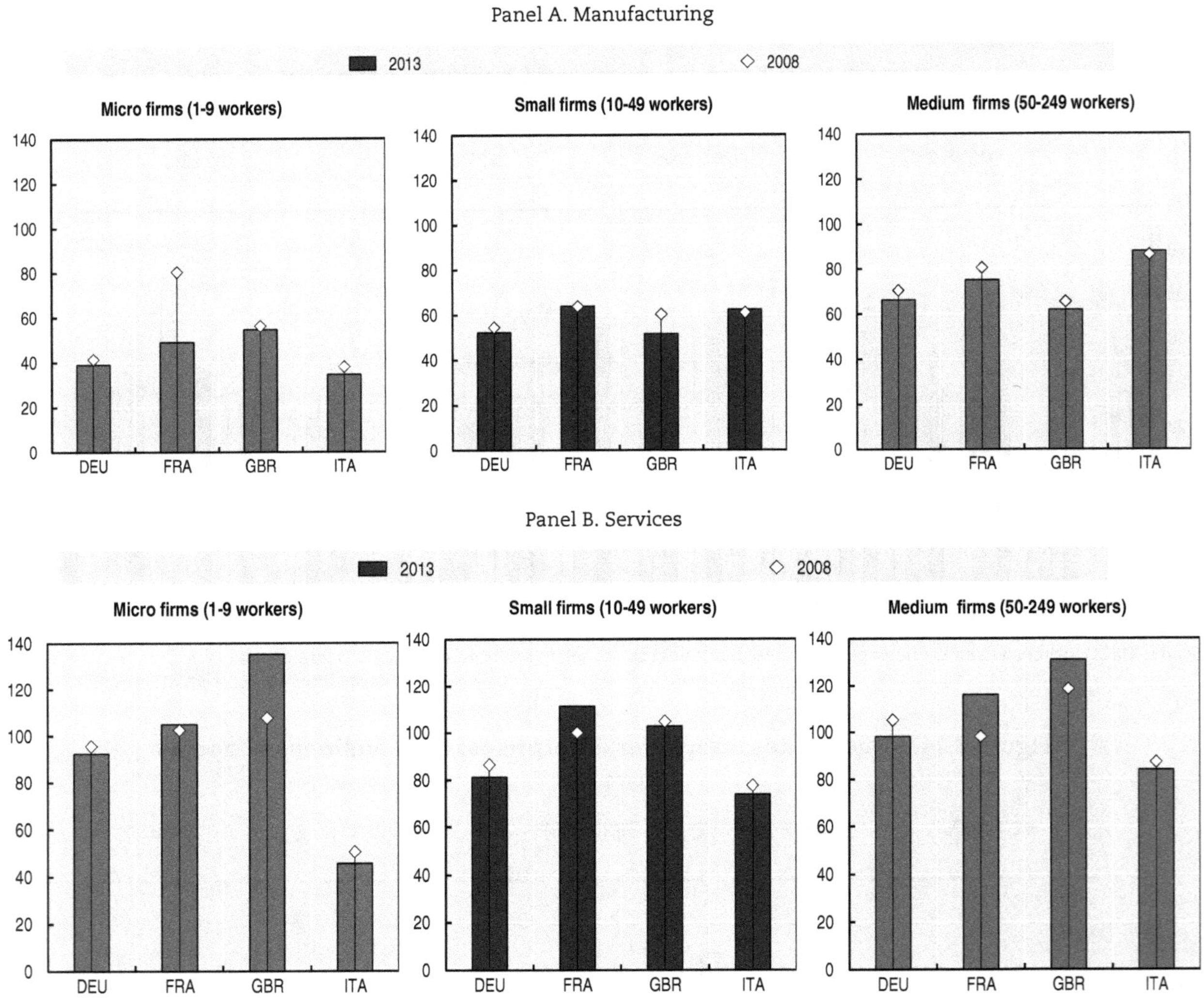

Source: OECD Structural and Demographic Business Statistics (database), *http://dx.doi.org/10.1787/sdbs-data-en.*

StatLink http://dx.doi.org/10.1787/888933346302

Current challenges in productivity measurement

Productivity measurement has long been a matter of considerable interest. There are a number of difficulties in accurately measuring productivity that can impact on recorded estimates and, in addition, impair international comparability, calling for a careful interpretation of currently available productivity measures. These difficulties manifest themselves both in the measurement of the factors of production, capital and labour, and in measures of output. The following sections set out these issues and highlight the potential impact that mis-measurement has on recorded estimates of productivity.

Labour

Hours worked vs head-counts

Conceptually, the volume of labour input reflects the time, effort and skills (quality) of the workforce employed in the production process. Ignoring for now quality differences in labour, labour input should in theory be measured as the total number of hours actually worked. Simple head-counts are not able to fully reflect the actual labour input as they are not able to adjust for differences in the relative shares of part and full-time employment, or indeed shifts in these shares that have marked labour markets in recent years. Nor are head-count figures able to account for other factors such as changes in statutory hours and absences from work, which reveals significant differences in nearly all economies (Figure 1.16).

Figure 1.16. **Labour productivity growth, 2009-14**

Total economy percentage change at annual rate

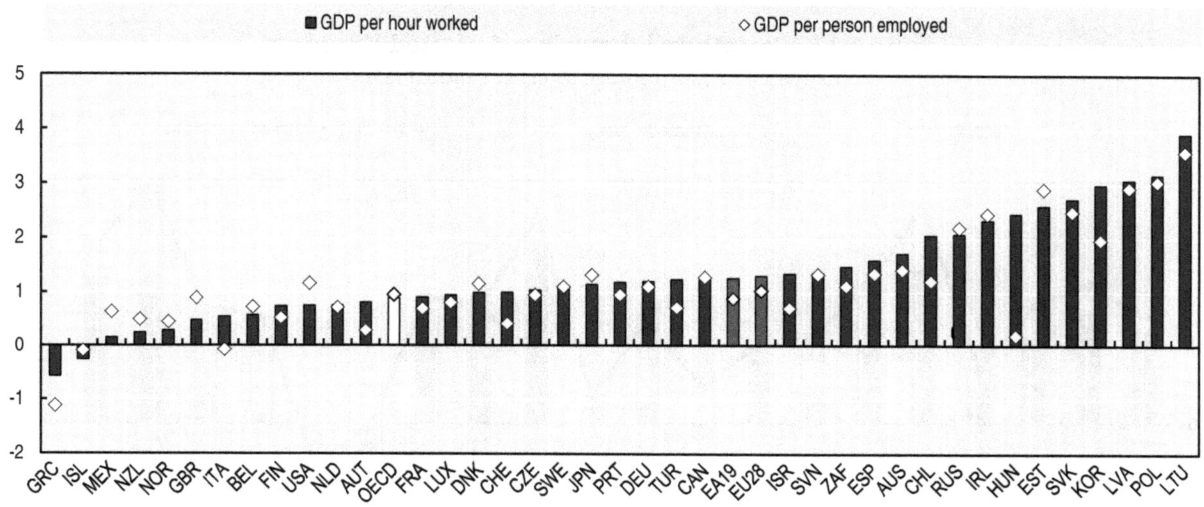

Source: OECD Productivity Statistics (database), *http://dx.doi.org/10.1787/pdtvy-data-en*, February 2016.

StatLink http://dx.doi.org/10.1787/888933346319

Adjusting for quality of labour

The effective quantity of labour depends not only on total hours worked or total number of persons employed but also on the characteristics (notably skills) of those performing the work. Conventional measures of productivity however are rarely able to account for these characteristics, meaning that they treat workers as perfect substitutes. For example, an hour worked by a highly-experienced doctor and an hour worked by student in a fast-food restaurant are treated as equal amounts of labour.

Evaluating skills and their productivity is however non-trivial, for example there would be little reason to expect significant differences in productivity between the doctor and the student if they both worked in the fast-food restaurant. Typically, studies have measured the quality of labour by identifying a number of characteristics such as industry worked in, occupation, educational attainment, or age and weighted them with their relative wage (Jorgenson et al., 1987; Bureau of Labor Statistics, 1993; Schwerdt and Turunen, 2008; O'Mahony et al., 2009). In recent years many national statistical offices have computed estimates of labour quality (e.g. Australia, Canada, New Zealand, the United Kingdom, the United States). All these studies rely on a cross-classification of hours worked by observed worker characteristics weighted with measures of average labour compensation shares attributable to each worker group. Most studies use predicted wages (based on wage differentials due to the selected labour characteristics and not to other factors) to determine the weights. Growth in labour quality is then estimated as the difference between the growth rate of quality-adjusted labour input and the change in total hours worked.

Accounting for the composition of the work force can alter the measured contributions to economic growth and provides the basis for a better understanding of conventional productivity measures. For example, the evidence points strongly to counter-cyclical movements in conventional measures of labour productivity and economic growth. During periods of strong growth the labour share of low-skilled workers tends to increase as firms reduce their skill requirements to expand production, resulting in downward pressures on labour quality; Figure 1.17 illustrates this for the United Kingdom.

Figure 1.17. **Growth in labour input, United Kingdom**

Total economy, percentage change at annual rate

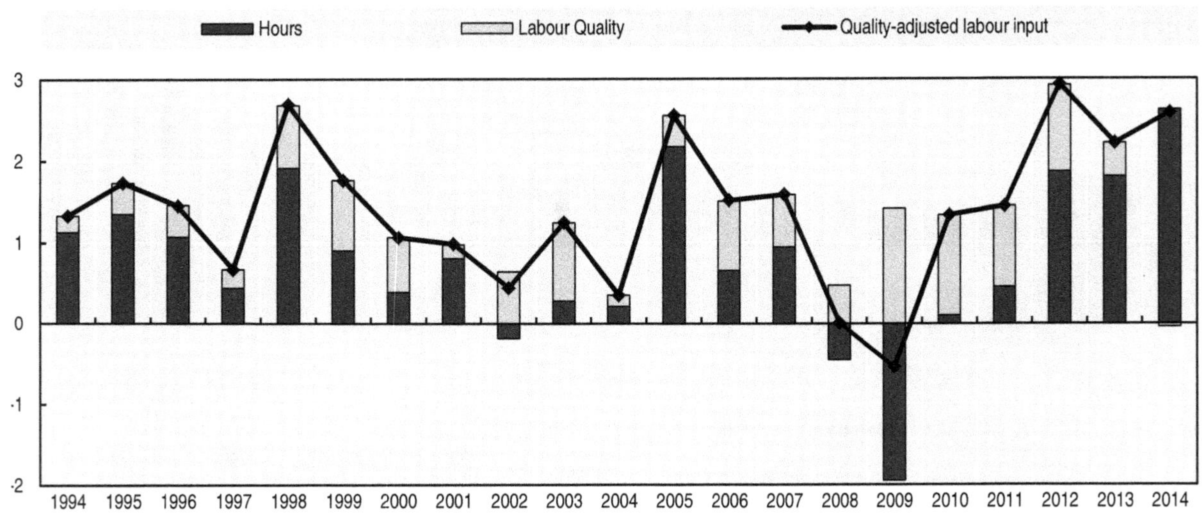

Source: UK Office for National Statistics.

StatLink http://dx.doi.org/10.1787/888933346329

More subtle questions regarding labour measurement include the treatment of (often increasing) commuting time to work as labour input or the fact that workers with zero hour contracts may be spending time on stand-by.

Capital

Comprehensive productivity estimates require exhaustive coverage of capital assets. But achieving exhaustive coverage in all countries remains elusive, partly by design in the SNA which only recognises as assets certain categories. Where coverage is not exhaustive this will necessarily impact directly on estimates of multifactor productivity.

Non-produced assets

Standard measures of multifactor productivity growth often ignore the contribution of the depletion or use of domestic subsoil assets (e.g. oil, gas, copper, lead) and land. However, income generated by these assets is captured in gross domestic value added.

It has been shown that the direction of the adjustment in traditional measures of multifactor productivity, when accounting for subsoil assets, depends on the change in the rate and value of subsoil asset extraction relative to other factor inputs (Brandt, Schreyer and Zipperer, 2013). Analysis at the industry level demonstrated less pronounced declines in the MFP of the mining sector in Australia when accounting for the contribution of subsoil assets (Argento and Burnell, 2013). MFP measures can also be enhanced on the output side by correcting GDP for undesirable output, i.e. emissions (Brandt, Schreyer and Zipperer, 2014). In a number of cases, this leads to an *upward* adjustment of measured productivity when undesirable outputs grow less quickly (or decline faster) than desirable outputs.

Knowledge-based assets

The SNA recognises a number of intellectual property assets: research and development expenditures, software and databases, mineral exploration costs, and artistic and literary originals. But these are not the only forms of knowledge-based assets that can contribute to growth. It is widely recognised that assets such as organisational capital, brand equity, training, or design can all play an important role (Corrado, Hulten and Sichel, 2005, 2009; OECD, 2013). Their exclusion from the production boundary of the SNA is not based on conceptual grounds but rather on the very practical difficulties involved in measuring them in a comparable and meaningful way across countries.

Indeed, measurement of intellectual property products already included in the SNA is far from trivial. New international measurement guidance (for instance, OECD 2010) has greatly improved international comparability, although scope for continued improvement remains, noticeably in measuring price changes, which struggle to capture changes in quality, in no small part reflecting the often unique nature of the assets, but also in determining depreciation rates for different categories of assets (see also "Output" below).

A number of studies, including at the OECD, have conducted analysis that complements the SNA asset boundary through the inclusion of additional knowledge-based assets. Despite important measurement challenges there remains strong appetite among the international statistical community to develop improved and comparable methods that can have near universal (global) application. The effects on productivity growth of extending capital measurement to these assets are hard to predict as both capital input and output are altered by their inclusion.

Also, for multinational firms in particular, the benefits from these assets, especially organisational capital, design, brand, can accrue to any or all of the affiliates. But the methods that are used to estimate the value of these assets typically allocate all value to the country where the asset creation occurred (such as R&D departments in headquarters). However, from a standpoint of measuring productivity, capital services should be measured where they enter the production process. The correct accounting approach would necessarily need to adjust value added in all parties, a difficult venture for which data are presently lacking.

Profit shifting and globalisation

The potential disconnect between capital on one side and recorded output and value added on the other, referred to above, carries even greater weight in the light of tax optimisation by MNEs as profits are shifted between jurisdictions without any recorded transfer or shifting of the assets, such as brands, and R&D, generating that production.

The international statistics community, starting with the OECD Task Force on Research and Development and subsequently UNECE Task Forces on Globalisation in the National Accounts and Global Production, have for a number of years strived to introduce clarity, with a key focus on attempting to ensure alignment with the principles of economic ownership (i.e. who runs the risks and receives the rewards) but the current situation remains a work-in-progress with all Task Forces calling for further work to be conducted.

Unlike many of the issues raised above and below, the question is not necessarily that the related flows (payments and receipts) from the use of the assets are not recorded in the accounts, but whether the flows align with national accounts concepts of *economic ownership*, rather than *legal ownership*. This means that current estimates, and comparability, of GDP across countries will be affected as too will be productivity.

Output

As a general remark, any mis-measurement of output will have direct consequences on measures of productivity. It is well known that the measurement of the volume of output is particularly challenging in the area of services, where price indices that can capture quality changes, are crucial but often elusive, particularly for services. Significant efforts are however being made to improve this situation, for instance by OECD and Eurostat (2014). The following sections list specific areas that warrant special attention.

Non-market activities

The lack of information on market prices and the difficulties of measuring the output volume of health, education and public administration services constitute an important challenge for productivity measurement. In many OECD countries, these activities account for over 20% of total GDP. Any shortcomings in sector productivity measurement thus affect aggregate productivity measures. In some countries, the volume of these services is often estimated on the basis of inputs, meaning that output and input volumes are not independent of one another and implying zero productivity growth. That said, progress has been made in the development of output-based measures for health and education services that are independent of inputs (Schreyer, 2010). For activities of the general administration (e.g., providing security or delivering quality regulation for business or integrity in procurement), on the other hand, it is much harder to develop sound measures of output, for conceptual and empirical reasons.

For all non-market producers, the SNA specifically rules out the addition of an imputation for the cost of capital services in arriving at the total value of output, adding only a component for depreciation and not the opportunity costs or financing costs of capital. The main reason for this convention lies in the fact that any such imputation directly affects GDP and national income and that there is a broad spectrum of possible imputations. That said, few studies show alternatives for dealing with this complication (Jorgenson and Landefeld, 2006; OECD, 2009). From the perspective of productivity measurement, the asymmetric treatment of assets used in market and non-market production results in an incomplete estimate of capital inputs and an asymmetric treatment of the same asset, depending on the sector affiliation of the asset owner (Jorgenson and Schreyer, 2013). For analytical applications it may therefore be useful to deviate from the national accounts convention.

Financial services

A particular challenge concerning financial services relates to the imputed item, referred to in the System of National Accounts 2008 (2008 SNA) as Financial Intermediation Services Indirectly Measured (FISIM), which reflects the implicit service provided by banks for intermediation services (e.g. liquidity transformation, teller machines, etc.) where explicit charges are not typically made, and instead are recouped as the difference between a risk free reference rate and deposit rates, for depositors, and the difference between lending rates and the reference rate for borrowers. Significant efforts have been made in recent years to improve international comparability and estimation methods (ISWGNA, 2013), but challenges, particularly for prices, remain.

Digitalisation

The digitalisation of the economy has brought with it the provision of free services such as internet search capacity or contents available for free. Some authors have argued that this output is missing from GDP statistics, implying an under-estimation of production and possibly productivity. This is certainly an issue that impacts on notions of consumer surplus, and although it is clear that a more substantive investigation of the issue is warranted, at least to provide further guidance on how the accounting framework deals with these flows and whether the activities are correctly estimated in practice, the emerging consensus is that the conceptual accounting framework for GDP is not deficient in this respect (Ahmad and Schreyer, 2016).

One area where there has been considerable debate in recent years relates to the digital revolution, characterised in large part by new players such as AirBnB and UberPop and their new business models, creating new Business to Customer (B2C) and Customer to Customer (C2C) activities. These new models are clearly disruptive and some commentators have argued that they put in question traditional productivity measures by ignoring production and transactions among households.

However, apart from cases where new C2C models may create opportunities for fiscal evasion (and so under-declaration of output and indeed employment), there is no reason to believe that the arrival of these new models has necessarily caused new and significant systemic measurement problems per se. Certainly the output (fees, commissions, etc.) of the new coordinating players should be recorded in the national accounts.

Concerning C2C transactions, which resemble bartering transactions, such as house swapping, again there will be a disruptive impact on economic activity (e.g. on the hotel sector), with a potential impact on the related output recorded in the national accounts as the activity is not picked up, but this can be tempered by the fact that the accounts already impute an estimate of output for dwelling services where owners occupy their own dwellings. Moreover, for productivity estimates, the lack of recorded output will be further tempered by the fact that there will also be no recorded labour input.

That being said, digitalisation is beginning to raise more profound questions about the scope of the accounting framework. Models like UberPop and Cashierless tills are dependent on greater participation (labour input) on the part of the consumer, but the consumer's activity remains outside of the GDP production boundary. In effect, the new business models imply a partial shifting of a service activity to the final consumer. Indeed questions are also being raised about the participative role that consumers play in receiving free services (e.g. media) financed through advertising revenues (Nakamura and Soloveichik, 2015). The overall effect on welfare from a societal perspective remains to be fully explored: to the extent that consumers provide unpaid labour services, there may be some negative welfare effects. But new technologies and service agreements also greatly enhance consumer convenience, they permit quick and costless access to information and entertainment, and they improve individuals' search capacity and so generate positive welfare effects.

Prices

Adequately capturing price changes, and differentiating between pure price change and quality (volume) change remains a long-standing challenge. And with products, in particular services but increasingly also goods, becoming more unique via customisation, price comparisons that control for quality differences are more complicated. The *Eurostat-OECD Methodological Guide for Developing Producer Price Indices for Services* (OECD and Eurostat, 2014) provides detailed advice on this issue by product, highlighting a number of approaches that could be used for measuring price changes in specialised products (contract pricing, model pricing, component pricing, hedonic methods), but accurately measuring quality changes remains challenging. However, it is perhaps important to put the issue of "customisation" into its appropriate context when considering volume measures of GDP. The objective is to measure price *changes*, not the price *level* of the product. Consequently, proxy estimates that employ comparable price changes over comparable (non-customised) products may limit the scope of potential errors on volume and productivity estimates.

One characteristic of globalisation has been the significant increase in outsourcing strategies that have brought with them significant substitution between domestically produced goods and imports. In many countries, however, it is not possible to accurately capture the corresponding price changes, impacting on volume estimates of GDP and hence productivity (Reinsdorf and Yuskavage, 2014).

Going forward

From the above it is clear that a significant number of challenges remain both in improving our understanding of the drivers of productivity and in improving measurement of those drivers. These include, but are not restricted to, the measurement of human capital, skills, knowledge-based assets, the use of natural resources, and the digital economy, in particular the new business models, all of which form important strands of the OECD's statistical work programme. But, notwithstanding progress in these areas, the current indications are that measurement, or rather mis-measurement, is unlikely to fully explain the recent productivity slowdown and paradox. Trends in productivity growth across advanced economies suggest that the slowdown has been underway for decades, and only accentuated by the crisis, reflecting a mixture of structural and cyclical factors. Inefficiencies in the allocation of resources, such as skills mismatches, sluggish investment, lower growth in international trade and a decline in business dynamism all feature as possible suspects. But there is also concern that there may be more than just a casual relationship with the increase in income and wealth inequalities that have also been observed in recent decades across OECD economies. Indeed there is concern that the relationship may be causal, with inequalities creating unequal opportunities, trapping individuals in lower skilled and lower productivity activities, with lower earnings, higher job insecurity and poorer working conditions.

Addressing these issues and challenges, and in particular the links between productivity and inequalities, is at the heart of the 2016 OECD Ministerial Council Meeting, which recognises that promoting productivity growth while sharing productivity gains more evenly can create a virtuous circle to tackle inclusion gaps and foster in turn higher productivity.

Sources and further reading

Adalet McGowan, M. and D. Andrews (2015), "Labour Market Mismatch and Labour Productivity: Evidence from PIAAC Data", *OECD Economics Department Working Papers*, OECD Publishing, Paris, No. 1209, *http://dx.doi.org/10.1787/5js1pzx1r2kb-en*.

Ahmad, N. et al. (2003), "Comparing Labour Productivity Growth in the OECD Area: The Role of Measurement", *OECD Science, Technology and Industry Working Papers*, No. 2003/14, OECD Publishing, Paris, *http://dx.doi.org/10.1787/126534183836*.

Ahmad, N. and P. Schreyer (2016), "Measuring GDP in a Digitalised Economy", *OECD Statistics Directorate Working Paper*, forthcoming.

Andrews, D. and C. Criscuolo (2013), "Knowledge-Based Capital, Innovation and Resource Allocation", *OECD Economics Department Working Papers*, No. 1046, OECD Publishing, Paris, *http://dx.doi.org/10.1787/5k46bj546kzs-en*.

Andrews, D., C. Criscuolo and P.N. Gal (2015), "Frontier Firms, Technology Diffusion and Public Policy: Micro Evidence from OECD Countries", *OECD Productivity Working Papers*, No. 2, OECD Publishing, Paris, *http://dx.doi.org/10.1787/5jrql2q2jj7b-en*.

Andrews, D. and B. Westmore (2014), "Managerial Capital and Business R&D as Enablers of Productivity Convergence", *OECD Economics Department Working Papers*, No. 1137, OECD Publishing, Paris, *http://dx.doi.org/10.1787/5jxx3d441knr-en*.

Argento, L. and D. Burnell (2013), "Australian valuation of subsoil natural resources and their inclusion in productivity statistics", *OECD Working Party in National Accounts*, *www.oecd.org/officialdocuments/publicdisplaydocumentpdf/?cote=STD/CSTAT/WPNA(2013)6&docLanguage=En*.

Baily, M.N., J. Manyika and S. Gupta (2013), "U.S. Productivity Growth: An Optimistic Perspective", *International Productivity Monitor*, No. 25, Spring.

Brandt, N., P. Schreyer and V. Zipperer (2014), "Productivity Measurement with Natural Capital and Bad Outputs", *OECD Economics Department Working Papers*, No. 1154, OECD Publishing, Paris, *http://dx.doi.org/10.1787/5jz0wh5t0ztd-en*.

Brandt, N., P. Schreyer and V. Zipperer (2013), "Productivity Measurement with Natural Capital", *OECD Economics Department Working Papers*, No. 1092, OECD Publishing, Paris, *http://dx.doi.org/10.1787/5k3xnhsz0vtg-en*.

Brynjolfsson, E. and A. McAfee (2011), *Race Against the Machine: How the Digital Revolution is Accelerating Innovation, Driving Productivity, and Irreversibly Transforming Employment and the Economy*, Digital Frontier Press.

Bureau of Labor Statistics (1993), "Labor Composition and US Productivity Growth, 1948-1990," *Bureau of Labor Statistics Bulletin* 2426, Washington, DC.

Byrne D., J. Fernald and M. Reinsdorf (2016), "Does the United States have a productivity slowdown or a measurement problem?", *Brookings Papers on Economic Activity*, *www.brookings.edu/~/media/projects/bpea/spring-2016/byrneetal_productivitymeasurement_conferencedraft.pdf*.

Cowen, T. (2011), *The Great Stagnation: How America Ate All The Low-Hanging Fruit of Modern History, Got Sick, and Will (Eventually) Feel Better*, Dutton.

Corrado, C., C. Hulten and D. Sichel (2005), "Measuring Capital and Technology. An Expanded Framework", Measuring Capital in the New Economy, Carol Corrado, John Haltiwanger and Dan Sichel (editors), University of Chicago Press, 2005.

Corrado, C., C. Hulten and D. Sichel (2009), "Intangible Capital and US Economic Growth", *Review of Income and Wealth*, Series 55, Number 3.

Gordon, R. (2012), "Is US Economic Growth Over? Faltering Innovation Confronts the Six Headwinds", *NBER Working Papers*, No. 18315.

Haan, M. et al. (2014), "The Dutch Growth Accounts: Measuring Productivity with Non-Zero Profits", *Review of Income and Wealth*, Series 60, Supplement Issue.

Ho, M. and D. Jorgenson (1999), "The Quality of the U.S. Workforce, 1948-95", Kennedy School of Government, Harvard University, Cambridge, MA, Unpublished Manuscript.

ISWGNA – Inter Secretariat Working Group on National Accounts, *Task Force on FISIM, 2013.*

Jorgenson, D., F. Gollop and B. Fraumeni (1987), *Productivity and U.S. Economic Growth*, Harvard University Press, Cambridge, MA.

Jorgenson, D. and P. Schreyer (2013), "Industry-level Productivity Measurement and the 2008 System of National Accounts", *Review of Income and Wealth*, Vol. 59.

Landefeld, S., D. Jorgenson and W. Norhaus (eds.) (2006), *A New Architecture for the U.S. National Accounts. Chicago*, University of Chicago Press.

Nakamura, L.I. and R.H. Soloveichik (2015); "Valuing 'Free' Media Across Countries in GDP"; *Federal Reserve Bank of Philadelphia Working Paper* No. 15-25.

OECD (2015a), *The Future of Productivity*, OECD Publishing, Paris, *http://dx.doi.org/10.1787/9789264248533-en.*

OECD (2015b), *OECD Science, Technology and Industry Scoreboard 2015: Innovation for growth and society*, OECD Publishing, Paris, *http://dx.doi.org/10.1787/sti_scoreboard-2015-en.*

OECD (2013), *OECD Skills Outlook 2013: First Results from the Survey of Adult Skills*, OECD Publishing, Paris, *http://dx.doi.org/10.1787/9789264204256-en.*

OECD-WTO (2012), "Trade in Value Added: Concepts, Methodologies and Challenges", *www.oecd.org/sti/ind/49894138.pdf.*

OECD (2010), *Handbook on Defining Capital Measures of Intellectual Property Products*; OECD Publishing, Paris, *www.oecd.org/std/na/44312350.pdf.*

OECD (2009) *Measuring Capital – OECD Manual 2009: Second edition*, OECD Publishing, Paris, *http://dx.doi.org/10.1787/9789264068476-en.*

OECD and Eurostat (2014), *Eurostat-OECD Methodological Guide for Developing Producer Price Indices for Services: Second Edition*, OECD Publishing, Paris, *http://dx.doi.org/10.1787/9789264220676-en.*

O'Mahony, M. and M. Timmer (2009), "Output, Input and Productivity Measures at the Industry Level: The EU KLEMS Database", *Economic Journal*, Vol. 119, Issue 538, pages F374-F403.

Reinsdorf, M. and R. Yuskavage (2014), "Offshoring, Sourcing Substitution Bias and the Measurement of US Import Prices", *BEA Working Papers*, WP2014-5.

Schreyer, P. (2010), "Towards Measuring the Volume Output of Education and Health Services: A Handbook"; *OECD Statistics Working Paper*, No. 2010/02, OECD Publishing, Paris, *http://dx.doi.org/10.1787/5kmd34g1zk9x-en.*

Schwerdt, G. and J. Turunen (2008), "Growth in Euro Area Labour Quality", *Review of Income and Wealth*, Series 53, Number 4.

Syverson, C. (2016), "Challenges to mismeasurement explanations for the U.S. productivity slowdown", *NBER Working Paper* No. 21974, *www.nber.org/papers/w21974.*

UK Office for National Statistics (2015), "Changes to National Accounts for Blue Book 2015: the deflation of investment in software".

OECD Compendium of Productivity Indicators 2016

Chapter 2

Economic growth and productivity

Size of GDP

Growth in GDP per capita

Gaps in GDP per capita

Labour productivity

Alternative measures of labour productivity

Alternative measures of income

Capital productivity and the role of ICT and intangible assets

Growth accounting

Multifactor productivity

Size of GDP

Gross Domestic Product (GDP) is the standard measure of the value of final goods and services produced in a country during a given period of time minus the value of imports. GDP per capita is a core indicator of economic performance and commonly used as a broad measure of average living standards or economic well-being.

Key facts

In 2014, the size of GDP for the OECD as a whole was about USD 49 700 billion based on current PPPs and the G7 countries accounted for almost 70% of that total. In the same year, GDP per capita was on average about USD 39 200 for the OECD area and about USD 10 700 for the BRIICS. However, there are large disparities in GDP per capita across countries within these geographical areas. Within the OECD, GDP per capita was above USD 50 000 in 2014 in Luxembourg, Norway, Switzerland, and the United States and less than half the OECD average in Mexico and Turkey. Amongst emerging economies, GDP per capita in the Russian Federation was more than twice the BRIICS average in 2014, while GDP per capita in India was slightly above 50%.

GDP growth slowed in most countries in the aftermath of the financial crisis. A sharp slowdown was observed in Finland, Greece, Iceland, Ireland, Spain, in most Eastern European economies and the Baltic States. At the same time, GDP growth has also eased in emerging economies, in particular, in Brazil, China, South Africa and, more significantly, in the Russian Federation, adding uncertainty to the global growth prospects given their large contribution to global trade and GDP growth.

Definitions

Countries measure the GDP in their own currencies. In order to compare these estimates across countries, they have to be converted into a common currency. The conversion is often made using current exchange rates but these can give a misleading comparison of the true volumes of final goods and services measured in the GDP. A better approach is to use purchasing power parities (PPPs), which are currency converters that control for differences in the price levels between countries and allow an international comparison of the volumes of GDP and the size of economies (Annex F).

Information on data for Israel: *http://dx.doi.org/10.1787/888932315602*.

Comparability

GDP measures are overall comparable across countries, although not all countries have yet implemented the latest international standards for the compilation of national accounts, the System of National Accounts 2008 (2008 SNA), which can have an impact on comparisons of GDP across countries. The measurement of the Non-Observed Economy (NOE) can also affect comparability as exhaustive coverage of production activities missed by the statistical system is difficult to achieve and the national estimates differ in their inclusiveness of non-observed activities. This can be a serious issue, particularly, in emerging economies.

Population estimates are comparable across countries. However, some care is needed in interpretation: for example Luxembourg and, to a lesser extent, Switzerland have a relatively large number of frontier workers. Such workers contribute to GDP but are excluded from the population figures, which is one of the reasons why cross-country comparisons of income per capita based on gross or net national income are also relevant.

Sources and further reading

OECD *National Accounts Statistics* (database), *http://dx.doi.org/10.1787/na-data-en*.

OECD (2002), *Measuring the Non-Observed Economy: A Handbook*, International Labour Office, Geneva 22/ IMF, Washington, DC/CIS STAT, Moscow/OECD Publishing, Paris, *http://dx.doi.org/10.1787/9789264175358-en*.

Figure 2.1. **Gross domestic product, current PPPs and current exchange rates**

The seven largest economies in the OECD, percentage of OECD total, 2014

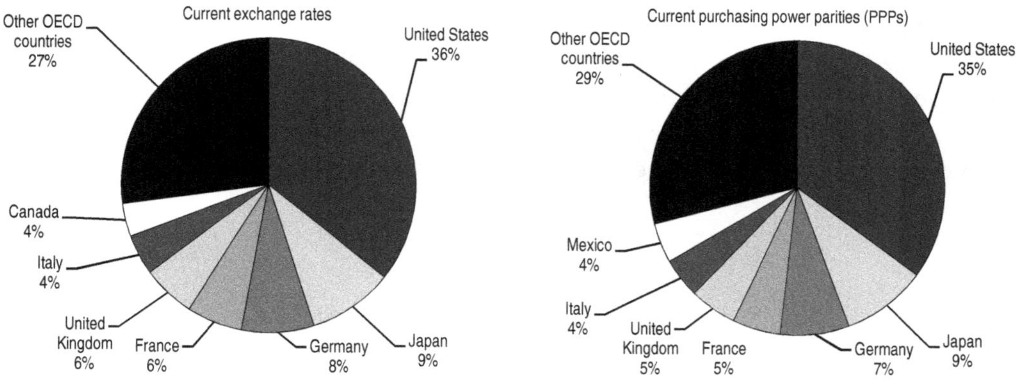

StatLink http://dx.doi.org/10.1787/888933346336

Figure 2.2. **Growth in gross domestic product**

Volume, percentage change at annual rate

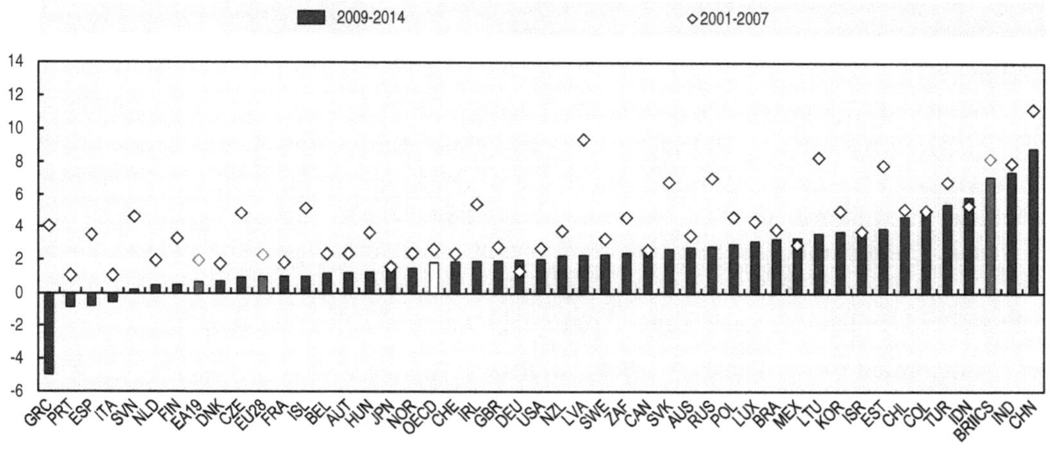

StatLink http://dx.doi.org/10.1787/888933346348

Figure 2.3. **GDP per capita**

US dollar per head of population, current prices and current PPPs, 2014

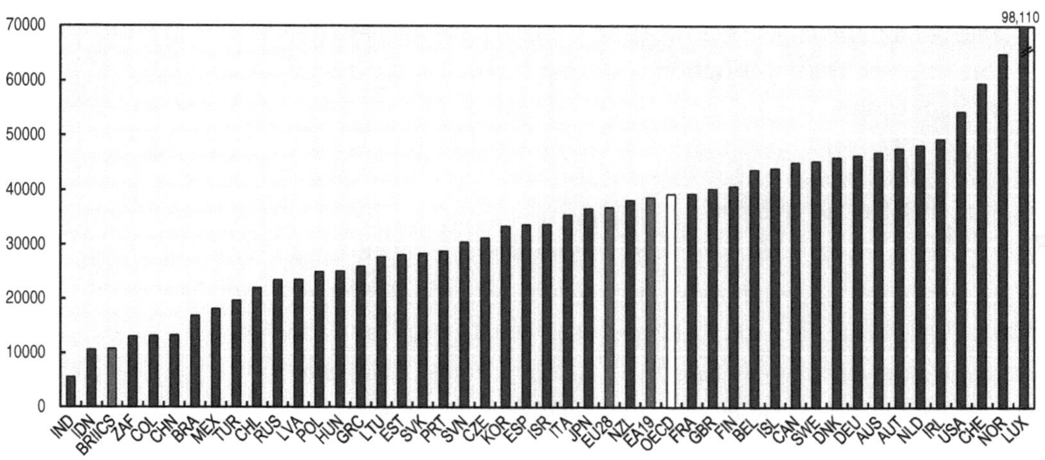

StatLink http://dx.doi.org/10.1787/888933346352

Growth in GDP per capita

Gross Domestic Product (GDP) per capita measures economic activity or income per person and is one of the core indicators of economic performance. Growth in GDP per capita can result from changes in labour productivity (GDP per hour worked) and labour utilisation (hours worked per capita). A slowing or declining rate of labour utilisation combined with high labour productivity growth can be indicative of a greater use of capital and/or of structural shifts to higher-productivity activities.

Key facts

Differences in GDP per capita growth across countries can be mainly attributed to differences in labour productivity growth, as labour utilisation has increased only marginally over the last 15 years. The picture has been more varied since the outset of the global crisis. In some countries, declines in GDP per capita resulted not only from slower labour productivity growth but also from substantial falls in labour utilisation rates, the latter reflecting declines in employment and average hours worked.

Definitions

Growth in GDP per capita is calculated using GDP and population series published in the *OECD National Accounts Statistics* (database). Labour productivity is measured as GDP per hour worked and labour utilisation as hours worked per capita. Total hours worked are primarily sourced from the *OECD National Accounts Statistics* (database). For some countries, however, longer time series and/or more recent estimates need to be derived from the OECD *Employment and Labour Market Statistics* (database), the *OECD Economic Outlook: Statistics and Projections* (database) and national statistical offices (Annex B).

Information on data for Israel: *http://dx.doi.org/10.1787/888932315602*.

Comparability

Most countries derive annual estimates of real GDP using annually chain-linked volume indices. However, China, India, Indonesia, Mexico and South Africa currently produce fixed-base volume estimates with the base year updated less periodically. The System of National Accounts 2008 (2008 SNA) recommends the production of estimates on the basis of annual chain volume series. These produce better estimates of growth as the weights used for the contribution of different goods and services are more relevant to the period in question.

Sources and further reading

OECD Economic Outlook: Statistics and Projections (database), *http://dx.doi.org/10.1787/bd810434-en*.

OECD Employment and Labour Market Statistics (database), *http://dx.doi.org/10.1787/lfs-data-en*.

OECD National Accounts Statistics (database), *http://dx.doi.org/10.1787/na-data-en*.

OECD Productivity Statistics (database), *http://dx.doi.org/10.1787/pdtvy-data-en*.

OECD (2001), *Measuring Productivity – OECD Manual*, *http://dx.doi.org/10.1787/9789264194519-en*.

Figure 2.4. **Contributions to growth in GDP per capita**

Total economy, percentage change at annual rate

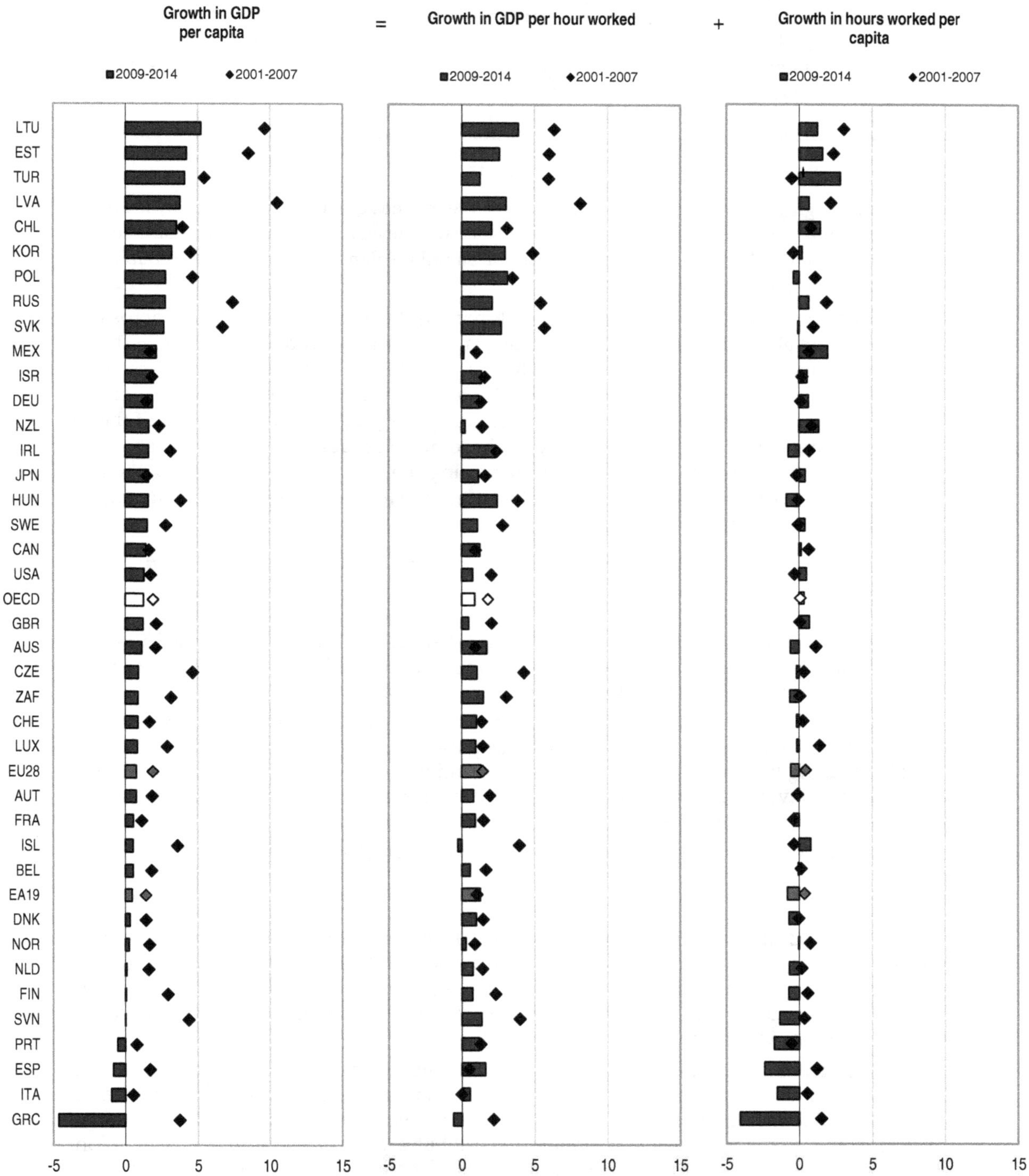

StatLink http://dx.doi.org/10.1787/888933346369

Gaps in GDP per capita

GDP per capita levels are typically used to compare living standards across countries. Differences in GDP per capita across countries can arise from differences in labour productivity levels and differences in labour utilisation (hours worked per capita). The latter can represent differences in unemployment, participation rates of the working age population and working hours per person employed.

Key facts

Very high growth rates in GDP per capita have meant that countries with initially lower GDP per capita levels converged towards average income levels in the OECD. This has been true for some OECD countries, in particular, for Estonia, Poland and the Slovak Republic, and for most emerging economies.

Nevertheless, in 2014, differences in GDP per capita remained significant across countries and also within the OECD area. GDP per capita was around 50% lower than the OECD average in Mexico and Turkey, while it was 2.5 times the OECD average in Luxembourg, 65% higher in Norway and 52% higher in Switzerland. Most of these differences in GDP per capita reflect differences in labour productivity levels. Half of the countries presented in Figure 1.6 (many of these non-European) show higher labour utilisation levels than the OECD average, narrowing their negative or reinforcing their positive gap in GDP per capita. This was notably the case for Iceland, Korea, Luxembourg, the Russian Federation and Switzerland.

Definition

GDP is measured as gross value added in market prices. Total hours worked used to calculate labour productivity measures are based on actual hours worked (Annex B). Labour utilisation is defined as actual hours worked per capita.

Data on GDP at current prices are sourced from the *OECD National Accounts Statistics* (database). For international comparisons, these data are converted to a common currency, US dollars, using *Purchasing Power Parities* (PPPs). Unlike currency exchange rates, the PPPs are currency converters that control for differences in the price levels between countries, making possible to compare absolute volumes across them (Annex F).

Information on data for Israel: *http://dx.doi.org/10.1787/888932315602.*

Comparability

For Chile, China, Colombia, India, Japan, Turkey and the Russian Federation the indicators are in line with the System of National Accounts 1993 (1993 SNA). For all the other countries, the indicators presented are based on the 2008 SNA. The 2008 SNA includes items such as the capitalisation of research and development (R&D) and military weapons systems which increase GDP levels (Annex D).

Population estimates are comparable across countries and are also sourced from the *OECD National Accounts Statistics* (database). However, some care is needed in interpretation as countries like Luxembourg and, to a lesser extent, Switzerland, have a relatively large number of frontier workers that contribute to GDP but are excluded from the population figures. In this context, cross-country comparisons of income per capita based on gross or net national income are also relevant.

Sources and further reading

OECD Productivity Statistics (database), *http://dx.doi.org/10.1787/pdtvy-data-en.*

OECD National Accounts Statistics (database), *http://dx.doi.org/10.1787/na-data-en.*

OECD (2001), *Measuring Productivity – OECD Manual, http://dx.doi.org/10.1787/9789264194519-en.*

Figure 2.5. **GDP per capita convergence**

Percentage change at annual rate (Y-axis); US dollars, current prices, current PPPs (X-axis)

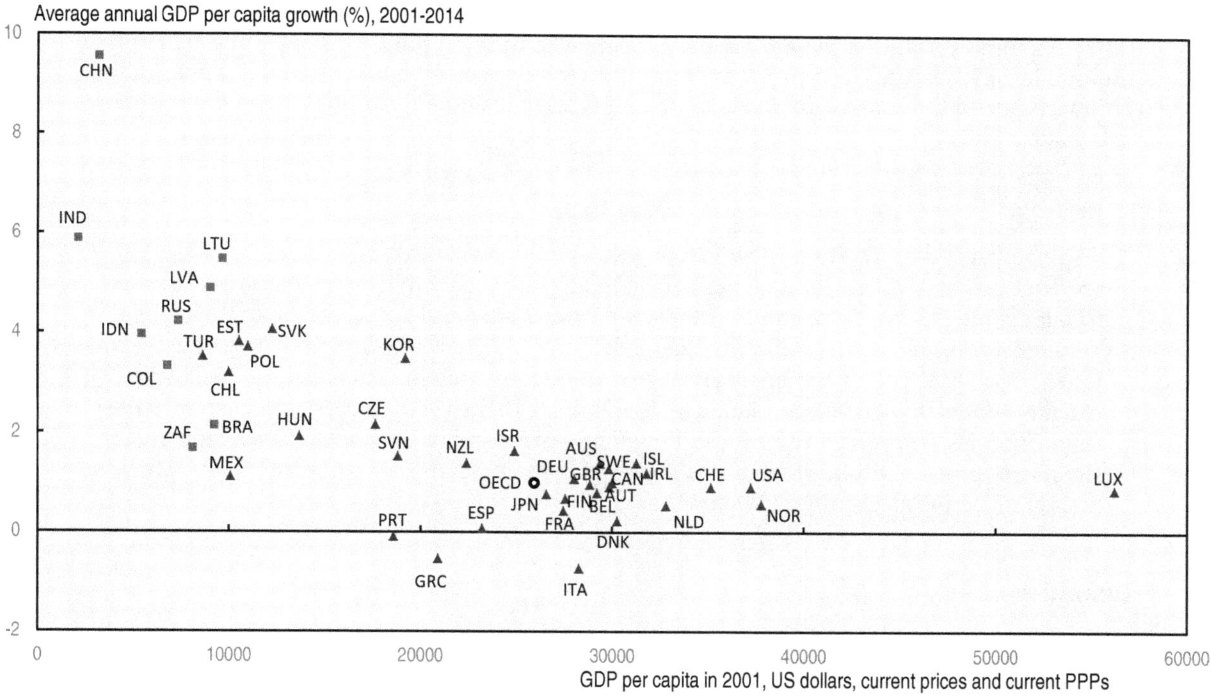

StatLink http://dx.doi.org/10.1787/888933346370

Figure 2.6. **Differences in GDP per capita levels, 2014**

Percentage differences vis-à-vis the OECD average, in current prices and current PPPs

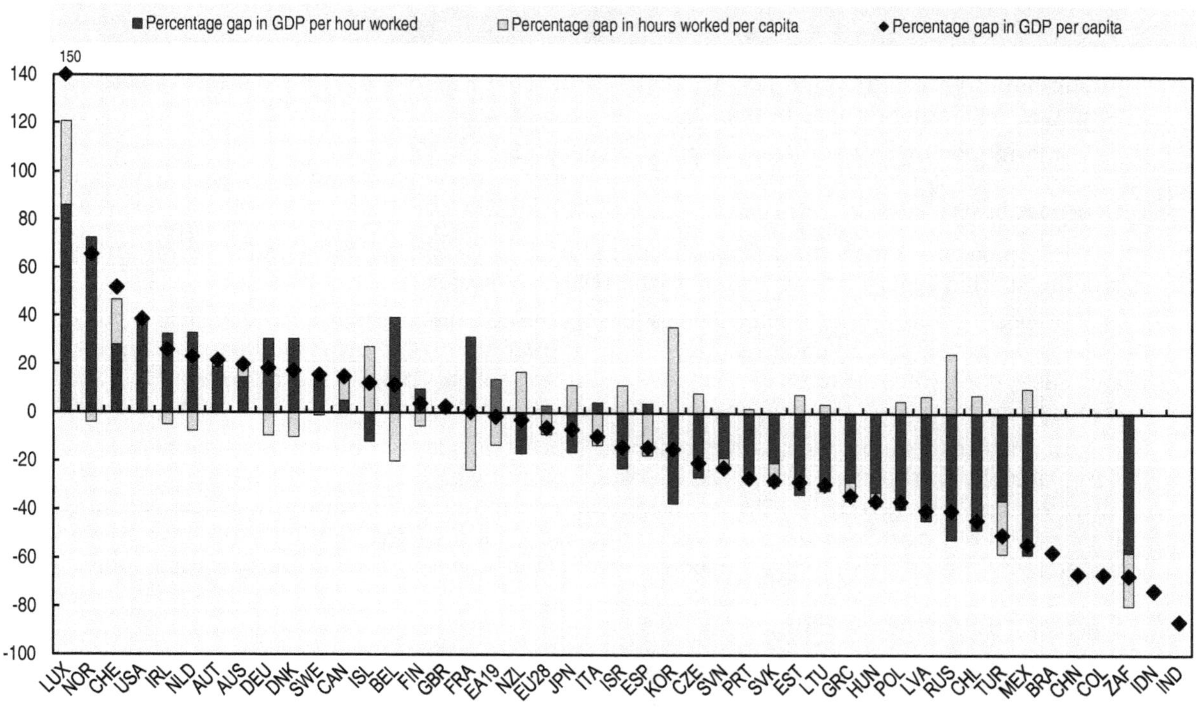

StatLink http://dx.doi.org/10.1787/888933346382

Labour productivity

Labour productivity is the most frequently computed productivity indicator. It represents the volume of output produced per unit of labour input. The ratio between output and labour input depends to a large degree on the presence of other inputs, such as physical capital, intangible fixed assets used in production and technical and organisational change. Labour productivity is a key dimension of economic performance and an essential driver of changes in living standards.

Key facts

In countries with relatively low labour productivity levels, stronger labour productivity growth over the last two decades has helped reduce the productivity gap. This is particularly true for some Eastern European countries, the Baltic States and Korea, although their labour productivity levels in 2014 still remained below the OECD average. And while productivity growth rebounded from the crisis lows, growth rates remained far below pre-crisis levels. Labour productivity growth remained relatively weak in the United States and in some large EU economies – Italy and the United Kingdom – compared with the OECD average and a significant productivity slowdown was observed in the Russian Federation and South Africa, mainly reflecting slackening GDP growth.

Definition

Labour productivity is defined as GDP per hour worked. GDP is measured as gross value added in market prices. For international comparisons of labour productivity levels, the series of GDP in national currency and at current prices are converted to a common currency, US dollars, using current *Purchasing Power Parities* (PPPs). Growth rates of labour productivity, instead, are based on measures of GDP in national currency and at constant prices.

In productivity analysis, and ignoring quality differences for the moment, labour input is most appropriately measured as the total number of hours actually worked, this is, effectively used in production, whether paid or not (System of National Accounts 2008, 2008 SNA, 19.47). Hours actually worked reflect regular hours worked by full-time and part-time workers, paid and unpaid overtime, hours worked in additional jobs, excluding time not worked because of public holidays, annual paid leaves, strikes and labour disputes, bad weather, economic conditions and other reasons (Annex B).

Information on data for Israel: *http://dx.doi.org/10.1787/888932315602*.

Comparability

GDP measures follow the 2008 SNA, except for Chile, China, Colombia, India, Japan, Turkey and the Russian Federation, which follow the 1993 SNA (Annex D).

In most countries, the primary sources for measuring hours actually worked are labour force surveys. However, several countries rely – only or in addition – on establishment surveys and administrative sources (Annex B). The use of different sources may affect the comparability of labour productivity levels but comparisons of labour productivity growth are less likely to be affected.

In practice, the effective quantity of labour input depends not only on the total number of hours actually worked but also on the education, working experience, business functions and other workers' characteristics. The measure of labour input used in this publication, i.e. total hours worked, does not account for the composition of the labour force and likely underestimates the effective use of labour in production affecting cross-country comparability.

Sources and further reading

OECD Productivity Statistics (database), *http://dx.doi.org/10.1787/pdtvy-data-en*.

Ahmad, N. et al. (2003), "Comparing Labour Productivity Growth in the OECD Area: The Role of Measurement", *OECD Science, Technology and Industry Working Papers*, No. 2003/14, *http://dx.doi.org/10.1787/126534183836*.

OECD (2001), *Measuring Productivity – OECD Manual*, *http://dx.doi.org/10.1787/9789264194519-en*.

Figure 2.7. **Labour productivity, 2014**

GDP per hour worked, total economy, US dollars, current prices and current PPPs

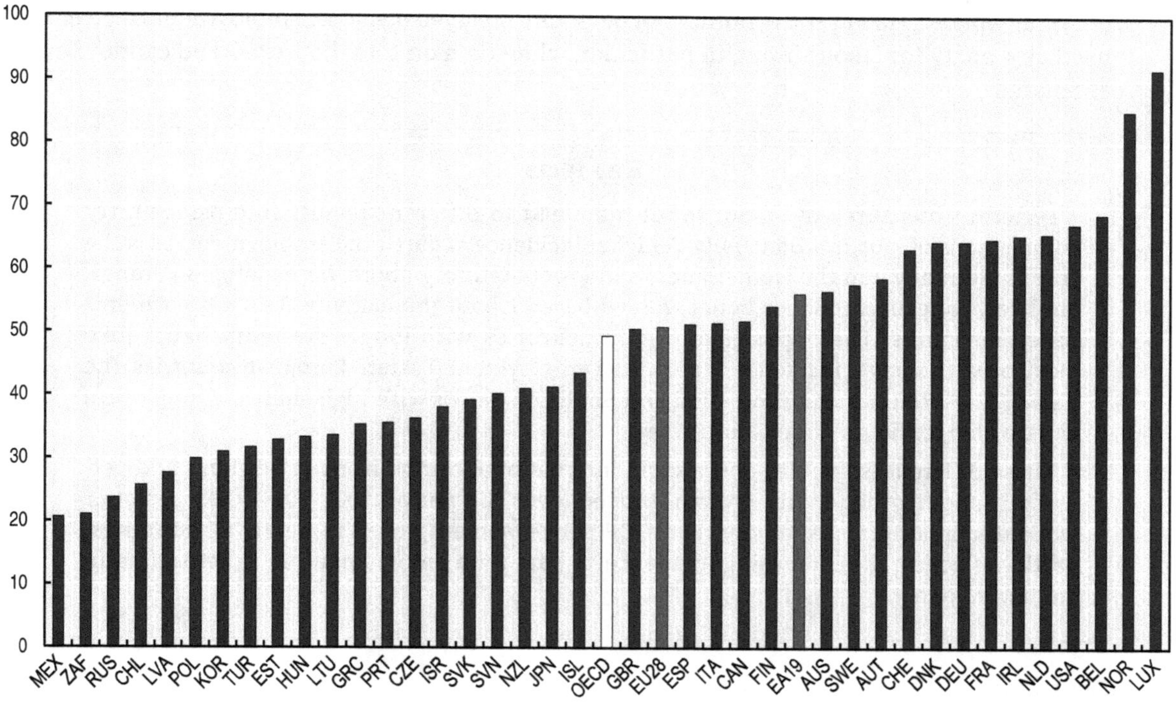

StatLink http://dx.doi.org/10.1787/888933346399

Figure 2.8. **Growth in labour productivity**

GDP per hour worked, total economy, percentage change at annual rate

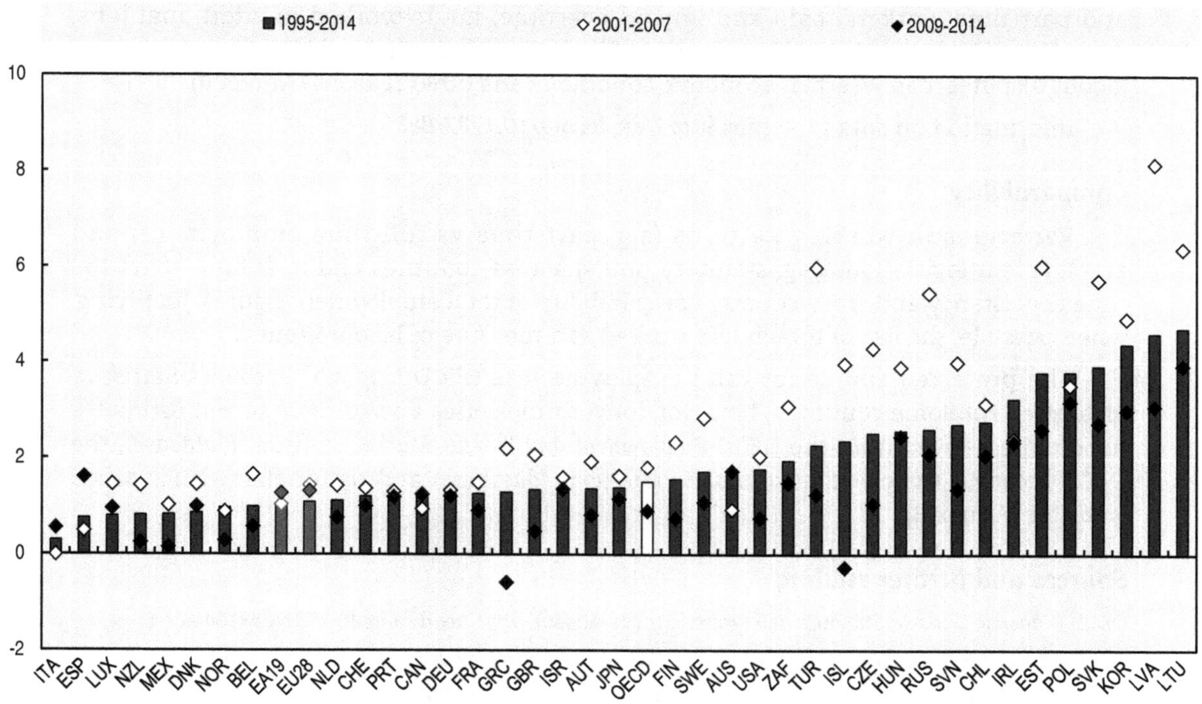

StatLink http://dx.doi.org/10.1787/888933346409

Alternative measures of labour productivity

Labour productivity is most appropriately measured as a volume of output generated per hour worked. However the number of persons employed (i.e. total employment) is often used as a proxy for labour input, in particular, when data on total hours worked cannot be estimated.

Key facts

Different measures of labour input may lead to different results in cross-country comparisons of labour productivity. A higher incidence of part-time employment, as is the case in Germany and the Netherlands, and lower statutory hours, for example in France, are likely to result in higher hours worked-based labour productivity than employment-based measures. The opposite is true in countries with longer statutory hours (like Mexico), with a lower incidence of part-time employment (Eastern European countries, the Baltic States, the Russian Federation and South Africa), or with high shares of employees working longer hours (Korea and Turkey).

These differences are also observed in international comparisons of per-hour and per-worker labour productivity growth. Indeed, over the period 2001-2014, GDP per hour worked increased more rapidly than GDP per person employed in nearly all countries, partly reflecting the increasing incidence of part-time employment and the decline in statutory hours.

Definition

Total employment is measured as the total number of persons engaged in production, including both employees and self-employed.

Hours worked refer to the total number of hours actually worked, this is, effectively used in production, whether paid or not. They reflect regular hours worked by full-time and part-time workers, paid and unpaid overtime, hours worked in additional jobs, excluding time not worked because of public holidays, annual paid leaves, strikes and labour disputes, bad weather, economic conditions and other reasons (Annex B).

Information on data for Israel: *http://dx.doi.org/10.1787/888932315602*.

Comparability

Variations in working patterns (e.g. part-time vs full time employment) and employment legislations (e.g. statutory hours) across countries and over time affect the time consistency and cross-country comparability of total employment figures, justifying, when possible, the use of total hours worked as a measure of labour input.

The preferred source for total employment is *OECD National Accounts Statistics (database)*. For some countries, however, longer time series and/or more recent estimates need to be derived from the *OECD Employment and Labour Market Statistics (database)*, the *OECD Economic Outlook: Statistics and Projections (database)* and national statistics office websites (Annex B).

Sources and further reading

OECD Economic Outlook: Statistics and Projections (database), *http://dx.doi.org/10.1787/bd810434-en*.

OECD Employment and Labour Market Statistics (database), *http://dx.doi.org/10.1787/lfs-data-en*.

OECD National Accounts Statistics (database), *http://dx.doi.org/10.1787/na-data-en*.

OECD Productivity Statistics (database), *http://dx.doi.org/10.1787/pdtvy-data-en*.

Figure 2.9. GDP per hour worked and GDP per person employed, 2014

As percentage of the OECD average (OECD = 100), current prices and current PPPs

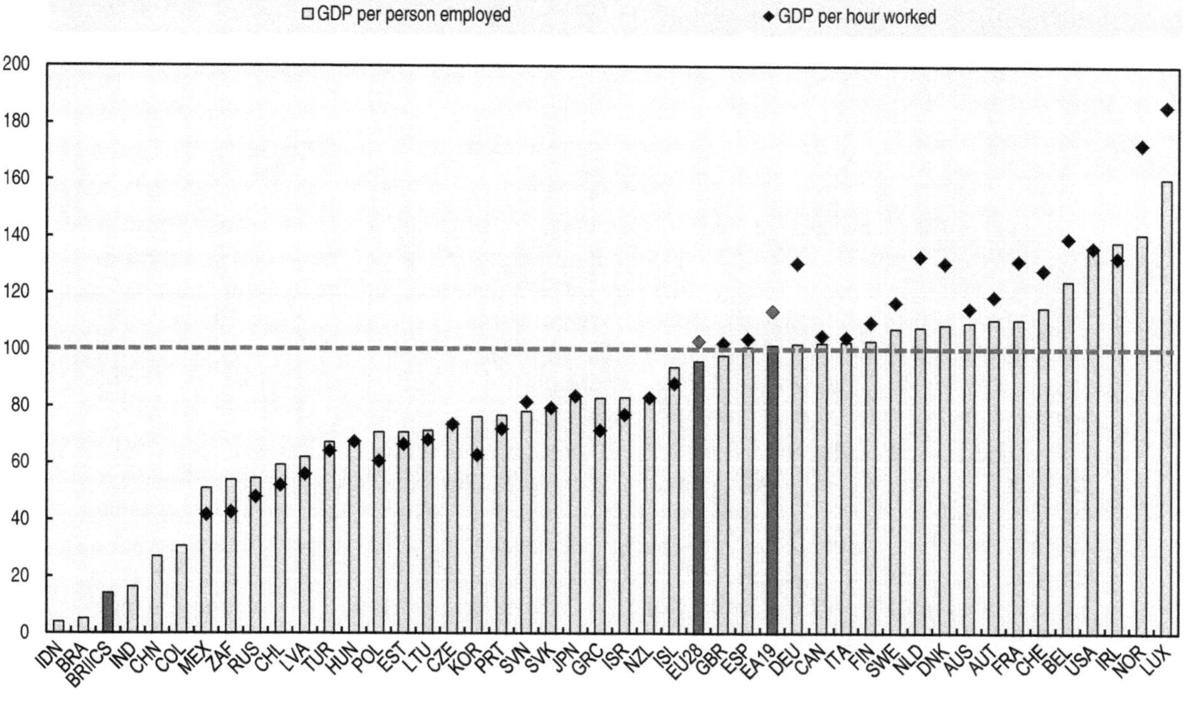

StatLink http://dx.doi.org/10.1787/888933346416

Figure 2.10. Growth in GDP per hour worked and growth in GDP per person employed, 2001-14

Total economy, percentage change at annual rate

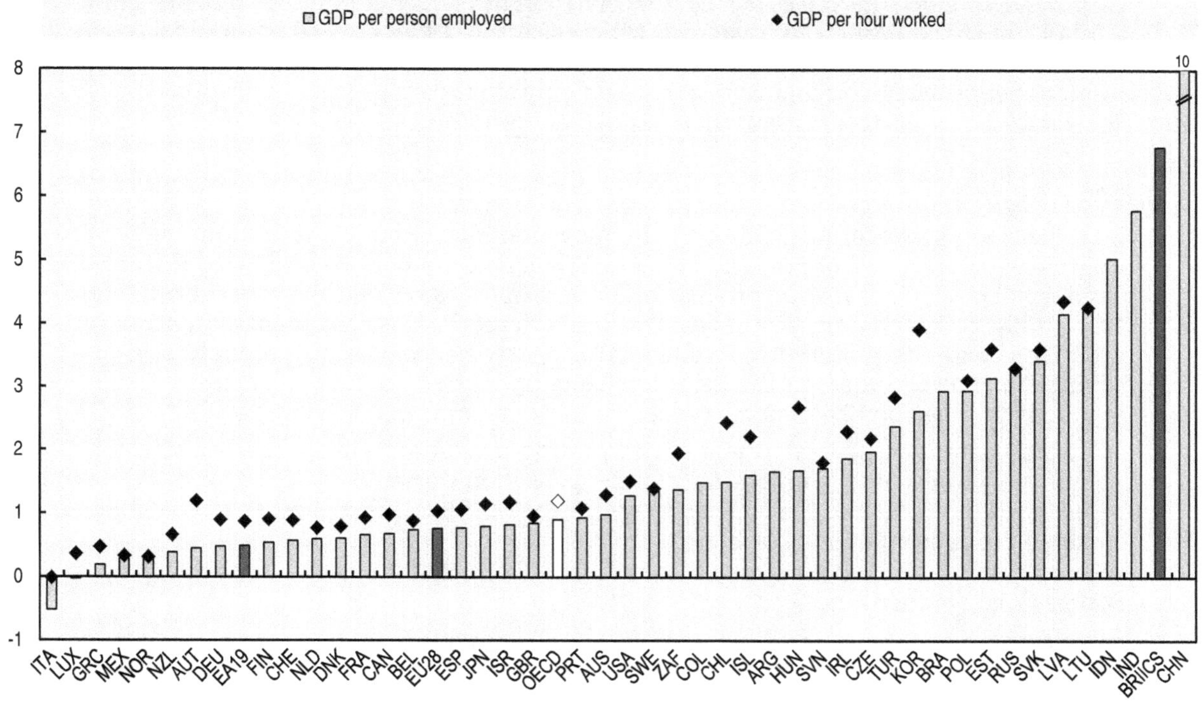

StatLink http://dx.doi.org/10.1787/888933346423

Alternative measures of income

In open economies with significant cross border flows of workers and, in particular, of property income, gross national income (GNI) may be more reflective of the income accruing in the country and available for future production. Indeed, GNI reflects the income received by citizens and companies of a particular nation located in the country and overseas.

Key facts

Most countries have small differences between their GDP and GNI measures, as income received from abroad nearly offsets payments made to the rest of the world. In countries with significant inflows of foreign direct investment, such as the Czech Republic, Ireland and Luxembourg, GDP exceeds GNI, as foreign affiliates engaged in local production repatriate the profits to parent countries. The opposite is observed in Denmark, Finland, Japan, Sweden and the United States, where parent multinational companies receive overseas profits from their affiliates abroad.

Productivity growth is relatively similar for most countries when measured on a GNI or GDP basis, although some noticeable differences exist. For example, over the period 2009-2014, Iceland experienced significantly higher growth in GNI per hour worked compared with GDP per hour worked, possibly reflecting decreasing (net) outflows of property income. On the other hand, in the same period, Latvia and the Slovak Republic recorded higher growth rates in GDP per hour worked than in GNI per hour worked, due to increasing (net) outflows of property income.

Definition

GNI is defined as GDP plus net receipts from abroad of wages and salaries and of property income plus net taxes and subsidies receivable from abroad. In most countries, net receipts of property income account for most of the difference between GDP and GNI. Property income from abroad includes interest, dividends and all or part of the retained earnings of foreign enterprises owned fully or in part by residents. Wages and salaries from abroad are those earned by residents who essentially live and consume inside the economic territory but work abroad. They also include wages and salaries earned by non-resident persons who live and work abroad for only short periods (seasonal workers).

Information on data for Israel: *http://dx.doi.org/10.1787/888932315602*.

Comparability

There are practical difficulties in the measurement of both international flows of wages and salaries and of property income. In practice, many flows related to the use of intellectual property assets are often recorded as property income flows between affiliates. This impacts directly on GDP levels but it also creates possible inconsistencies for productivity as the underlying intellectual property being used in production in one country may be recorded on the balance sheets of another country. Measures of labour productivity based on GNI in part 'correct' for these potential inconsistencies.

Some care is also needed when interpreting productivity in countries with high numbers of cross-border workers. Labour compensation earned by these workers will not be included in the GNI of the country in which they work but their hours worked will be included in the calculation of labour input.

Sources and further reading

OECD National Accounts Statistics (database), *http://dx.doi.org/10.1787/na-data-en*.

OECD Productivity Statistics (database), *http://dx.doi.org/10.1787/pdtvy-data-en*.

OECD (2009), *Handbook on Deriving Capital Measures of Intellectual Property Products*, *http://dx.doi.org/10.1787/9789264079205-en*.

Figure 2.11. **GDP and GNI per hour worked, 2014**

As percentage of the OECD average (OECD = 100), current prices and current PPPs

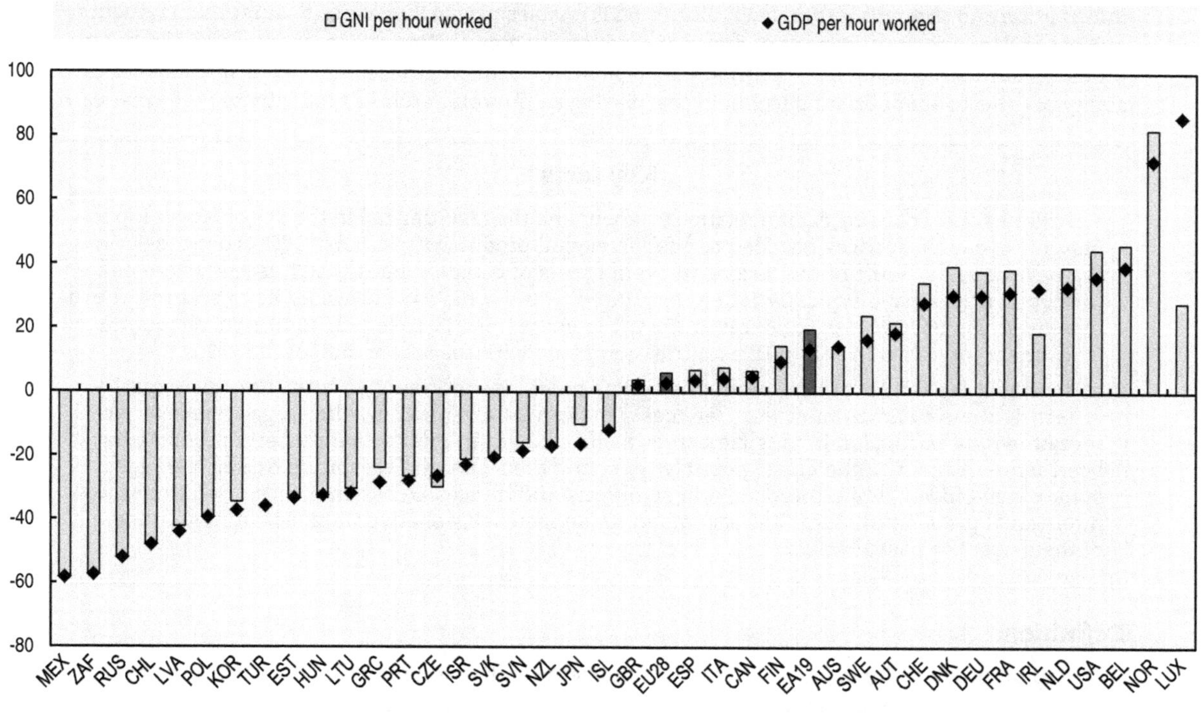

StatLink http://dx.doi.org/10.1787/888933346439

Figure 2.12. **Growth in GDP per hour worked and growth in GNI per hour worked**

Total economy, percentage change at annual rate

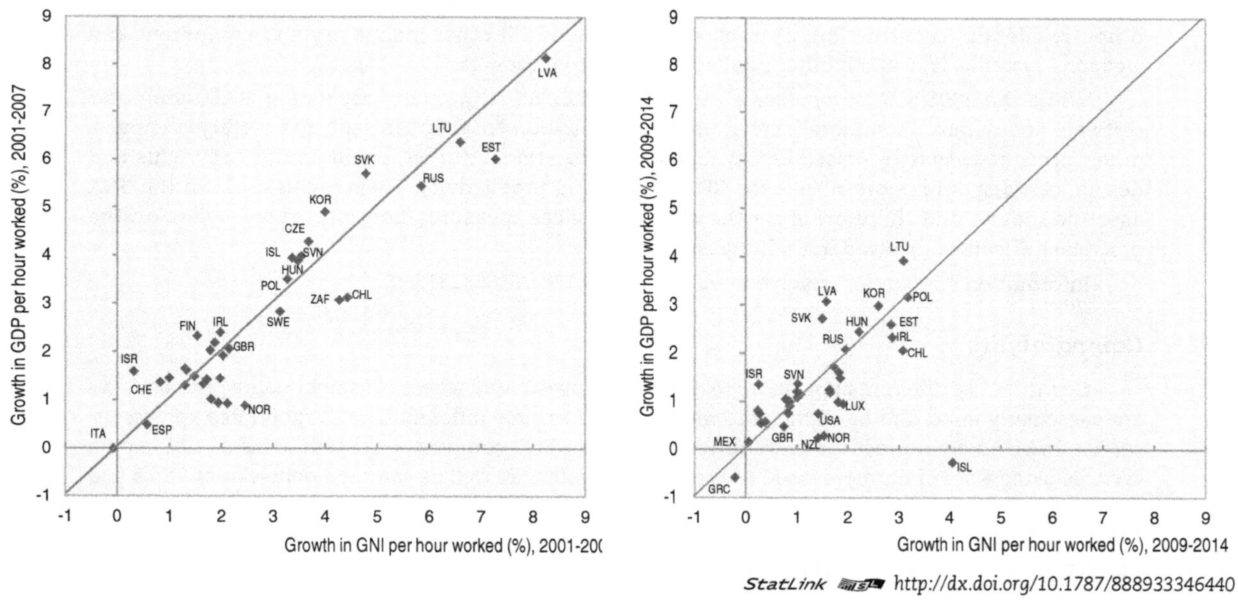

StatLink http://dx.doi.org/10.1787/888933346440

Capital productivity and the role of ICT and intangible assets

Capital productivity shows how efficiently capital is used to generate output. Investment in information and communication technologies (ICT) enables new technologies to enter the production process and is seen as an important driver of productivity growth. Investment in intellectual property products, such as R&D, not only contribute to expand the technological frontier but also enhances the ability of firms to adopt existing technologies, playing an important role in productivity performance.

Key facts

Declining costs of using capital relative to labour and the resulting fall in the use of labour input per unit of capital services have led to a fall in capital productivity in most OECD countries over the past 20 years. Some of the decline in overall costs of capital relates to ICT assets where new products' prices have typically fallen very rapidly, and which in turn may have spurred the increased use of ICT in production. In fact, the shares of ICT assets in total non-residential investment increased in nearly all countries compared with the second half of the 1990s.

However, the fall in capital productivity has been less pronounced after the crisis, partly reflecting the slowdown in capital services. This can be explained by the sluggish recovery of investment, in particular, in tangible assets, as investment in intellectual property products has been more resilient to the crisis, possibly reflecting their less cyclical nature due to the higher sunk costs. Indeed, while there are still significant differences across countries, investment in intellectual property products has accounted for an increasing share of total investment in most of them over the past 15 years.

Definition

Capital productivity is measured as the ratio between the volume of output, measured as GDP, and the volume of capital input, defined as the flow of productive services that capital delivers in production, i.e. capital services (Annexes A and C).

Series of gross fixed capital formation by asset type are used to estimate productive capital stocks and to compute an aggregate measure of total capital services in line with asset boundary of the System of National Accounts 2008 (*2008 SNA*). ICT capital includes: i) computer hardware; ii) telecommunications equipment; and iii) computer software and databases. Non-ICT capital includes: i) non-residential construction, ii) transport equipment; iii) other machinery and equipment and weapons systems; iv) R&D; v) other intellectual property products.

While the 2008 SNA recognises a number of intellectual property assets (i.e. R&D, computer software and databases, mineral exploration and evaluation costs and artistic and literary originals), other forms of knowledge-based assets such as organisational capital, brand-equity, copyrights and design, can play an important role for GDP growth and productivity. Their exclusion from the SNA asset boundary, and therefore from the capital services measures here presented, relies on the practical difficulties involved in their measurement.

Information on data for Israel: *http://dx.doi.org/10.1787/888932315602*.

Comparability

Countries use different approaches to deflate ICT investment, where constant quality price changes are particularly important but difficult to measure, and assume different depreciation rates and assets' service lives. To counteract for these differences, the OECD compute aggregate measures of capital services using a set of harmonised ICT investment deflators as well as common depreciation rates and average service lives for the different assets across countries (Schreyer, 2004).

Sources and further reading

OECD Productivity Statistics (database), *http://dx.doi.org/10.1787/pdtvy-data-en*.

OECD (2009), *Measuring Capital – OECD Manual*, *http://dx.doi.org/10.1787/9789264068476-en*.

OECD (2009), *Handbook on Deriving Capital Measures of Intellectual Property Products*, *http://dx.doi.org/10.1787/9789264079205-en*.

Schreyer, P. (2004), "Capital Stocks, Capital Services and Multi-Factor Productivity Measures", *OECD Economic Studies*, Vol. 2003/2, *http://dx.doi.org/10.1787/16097491*.

Figure 2.13. **Growth in capital productivity**

Total economy, percentage change at annual rate

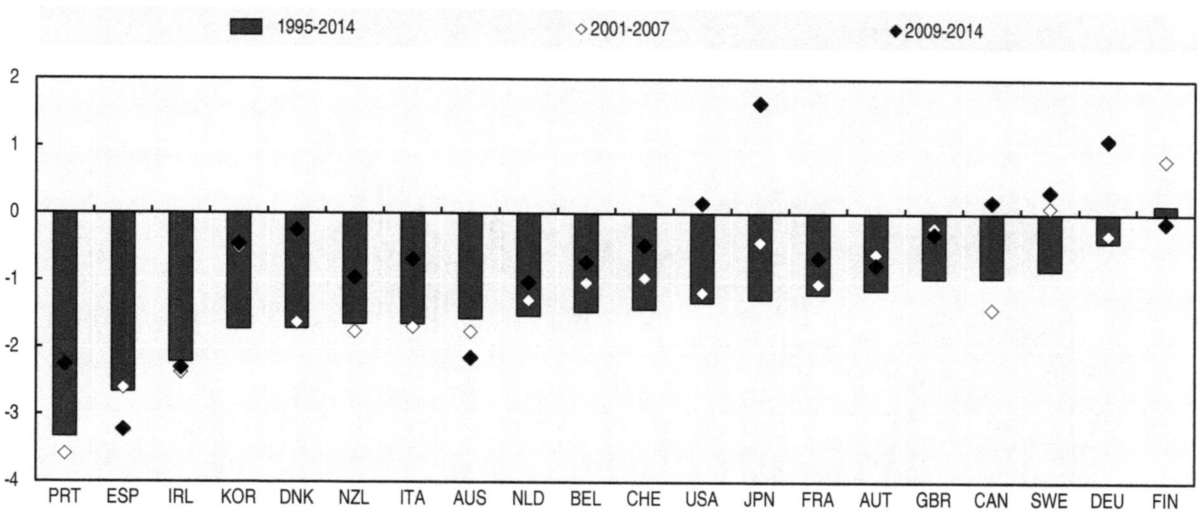

StatLink http://dx.doi.org/10.1787/888933346456

Figure 2.14. **Contributions of ICT and non-ICT capital to total capital services**

Total economy, percentage change at annual rate

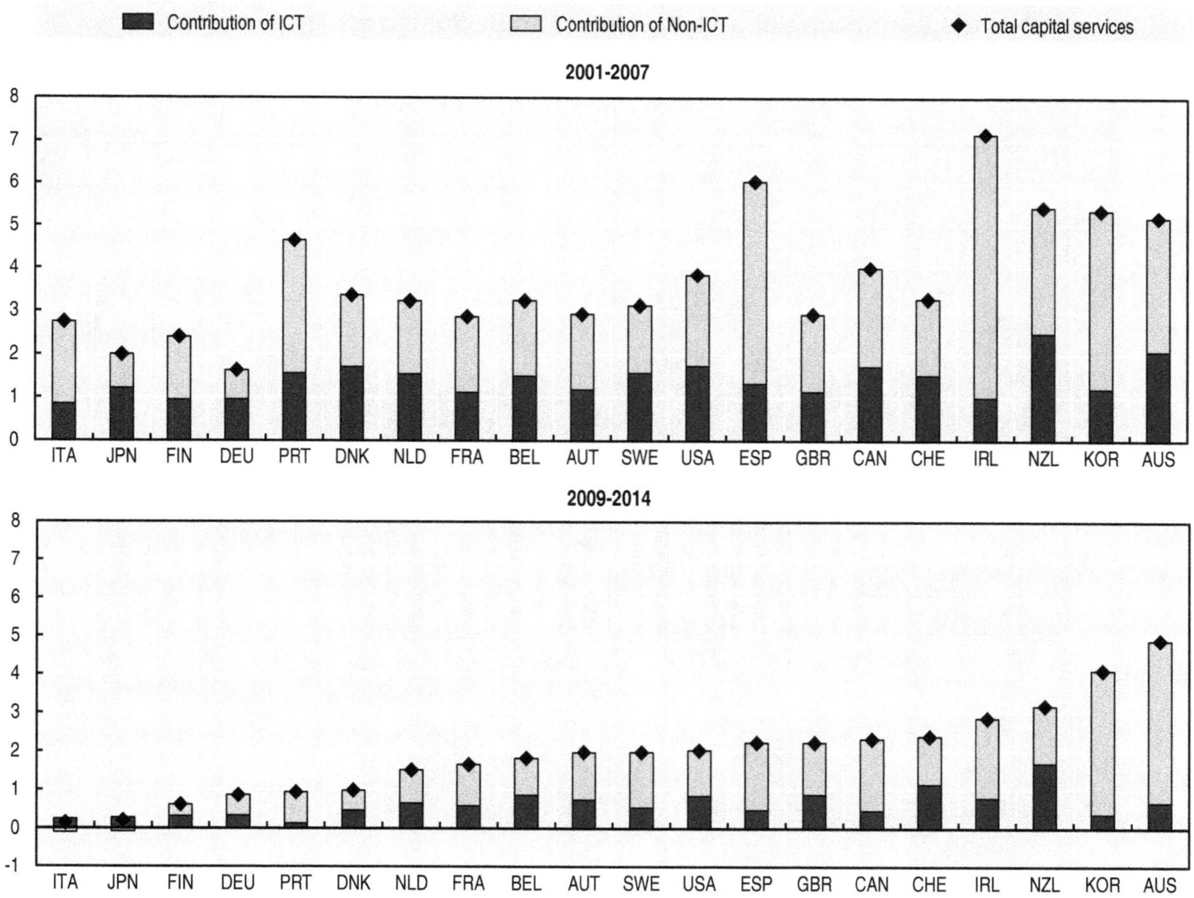

StatLink http://dx.doi.org/10.1787/888933346463

Figure 2.15. Share of ICT investment

Total economy, as a percentage of non-residential gross fixed capital formation

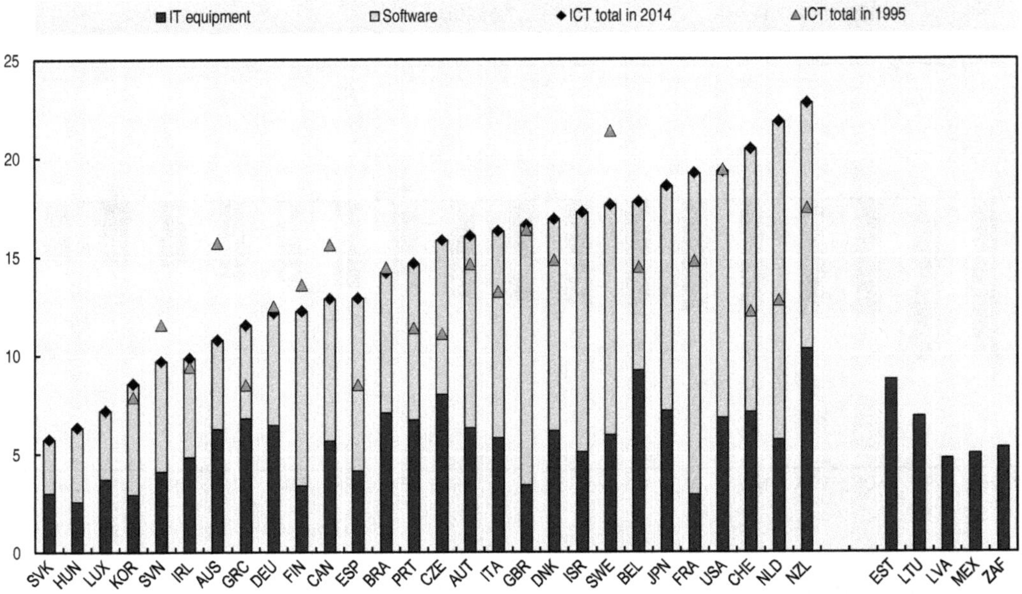

StatLink http://dx.doi.org/10.1787/888933346472

Figure 2.16. Share of investment in intellectual property products

Total economy, as a percentage of gross fixed capital formation

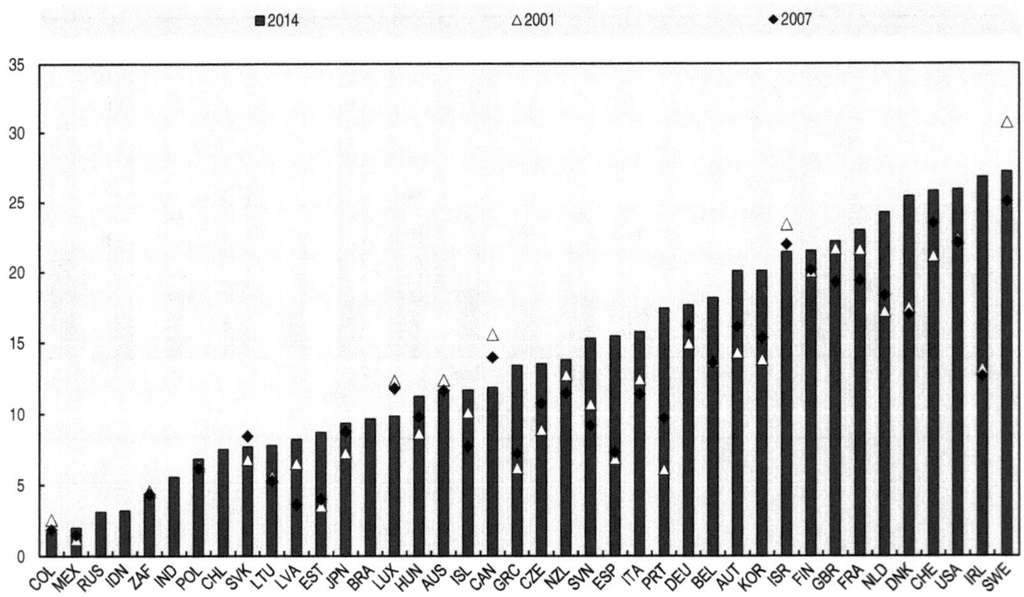

StatLink http://dx.doi.org/10.1787/888933346485

Figure 2.17. **Growth rate of investment in tangible assets and intellectual property products**

Total economy, percentage change at annual rate

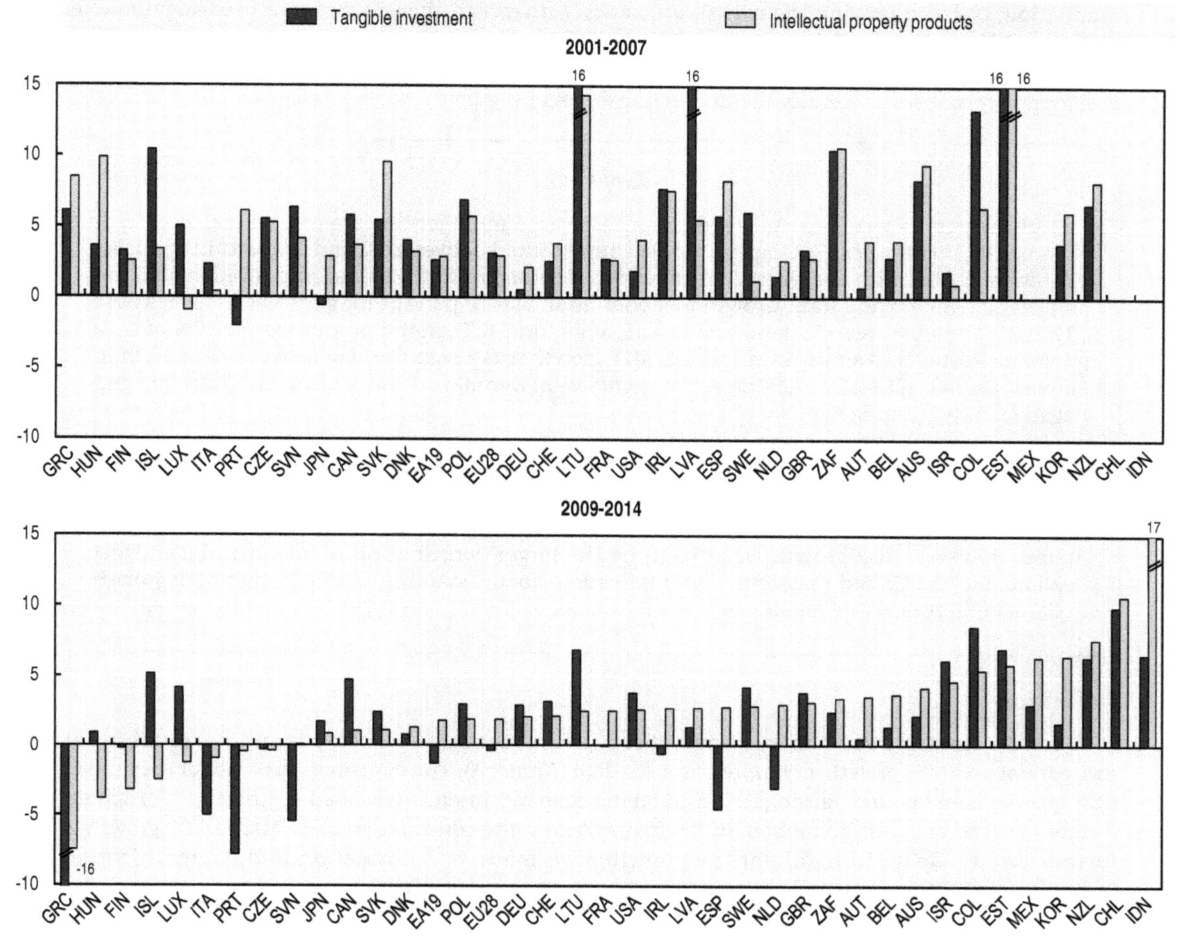

StatLink http://dx.doi.org/10.1787/888933346498

Figure 2.18. **Gross fixed capital formation by asset type, 2014**

Total economy, as a percentage of total gross fixed capital formation

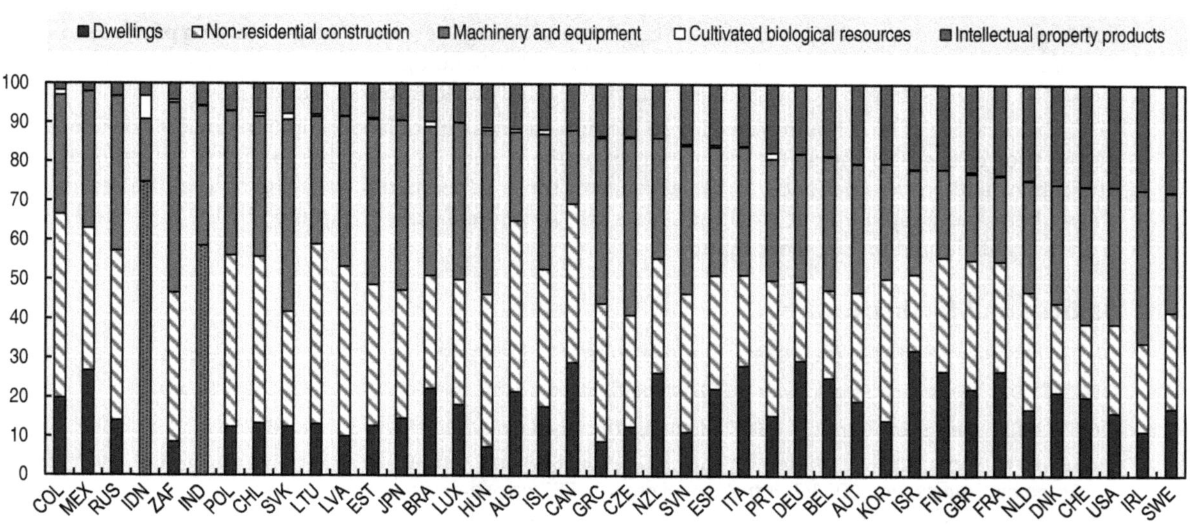

StatLink http://dx.doi.org/10.1787/888933346503

Growth accounting

Economic growth can be fostered either by raising the labour and capital inputs used in production, or by improving the overall efficiency with which these inputs are used together, i.e. higher multifactor productivity growth (MFP). Growth accounting involves decomposing total output growth, measured here as GDP growth, into these three components. As such, it provides an essential tool for policy makers to identify the underlying drivers for growth.

Key facts

Over the past 15 years, capital services and MFP accounted for the largest part of GDP growth in most OECD countries. ICT capital services represented between 0.2 and 0.6 percentage point of growth in GDP, with the largest contributions recorded in New Zealand and Sweden, and the smallest in Finland and Italy. Growth in labour input was important for very few countries over 1995-2014, notably New Zealand and Spain, while non-ICT capital accounted for 50% of GDP growth in Portugal. Over the same period, MFP growth was a significant source of GDP growth in Finland, Germany, Ireland and Korea, but negligible in Denmark, New Zealand and Portugal, and negative in Italy and Spain.

However, when contributions to GDP growth are analysed before and after the crisis, important differences arise. The slowdown in GDP growth over the period 2009-14 was driven by the negative contribution of labour input in Italy, Portugal, Spain, and, to a lower extent, Ireland, and by the smaller contribution of the MFP in Austria, Belgium, Finland, Korea and the United States. However, GDP growth was driven by the larger contribution of labour input in New Zealand and the United Kingdom, partly reflecting labour hoarding, and by higher MFP growth in Canada, Germany and Japan.

Definition

Total output growth can be decomposed into a labour input component, a capital input component and MFP growth, computed as a residual (Annex A). The contribution of labour (capital) to GDP growth is measured as the growth in labour (capital) input, multiplied by the share of labour (capital) in total costs of production. In the figures below, the contribution of capital to GDP growth is further broken down to highlight the contribution made by information and communication technologies (ICT) as compared with more traditional assets (non-ICT).

Comparability

In productivity analysis, the appropriate measure for capital input is the flow of capital services, this is, the flow of productive services that can be drawn from the cumulative stock of past investments in capital assets. Conceptually, capital services reflect a quantity, or physical concept, not to be confused with the value, or price concept of capital. To illustrate, the services flows of an office building are the protection against rain, the comfort and storage services that the building provides to personnel during a given period, rather than the value of the building. These services are estimated by the OECD using the rate of change of the productive capital stock (Annexes A and C).

The measure of total hours worked is an incomplete measure of labour input because it does not account for changes in the skill composition of workers, such as those due to higher educational attainment and work experience. In the absence of these adjustments, as is the case in the series shown here, more rapid output growth due to a rise in workers skills is captured by the MFP, rather than being attributed to the labour input.

Sources and further reading

OECD Productivity Statistics (database), *http://dx.doi.org/10.1787/pdtvy-data-en*.

OECD (2001), *Measuring Productivity–OECD Manual*, *http://dx.doi.org/10.1787/9789264194519-en*.

OECD (2009), *Measuring Capital – OECD Manual*, *http://dx.doi.org/10.1787/9789264068476-en*.

Schreyer, P. (2004), "Capital Stocks, Capital Services and Multi-Factor Productivity Measures", *OECD Economic Studies*, Vol. 2003/2, *http://dx.doi.org/10.1787/eco_studies-v2003-art11-en*.

Wölfl, A. and D. Hajkova (2007), "Measuring Multifactor Productivity Growth", *OECD Science, Technology and Industry Working Papers*, No. 2007/05, *http://dx.doi.org/10.1787/246367010342*.

Figure 2.19. **Contributions to GDP growth**

Total economy, annual percentage point contribution

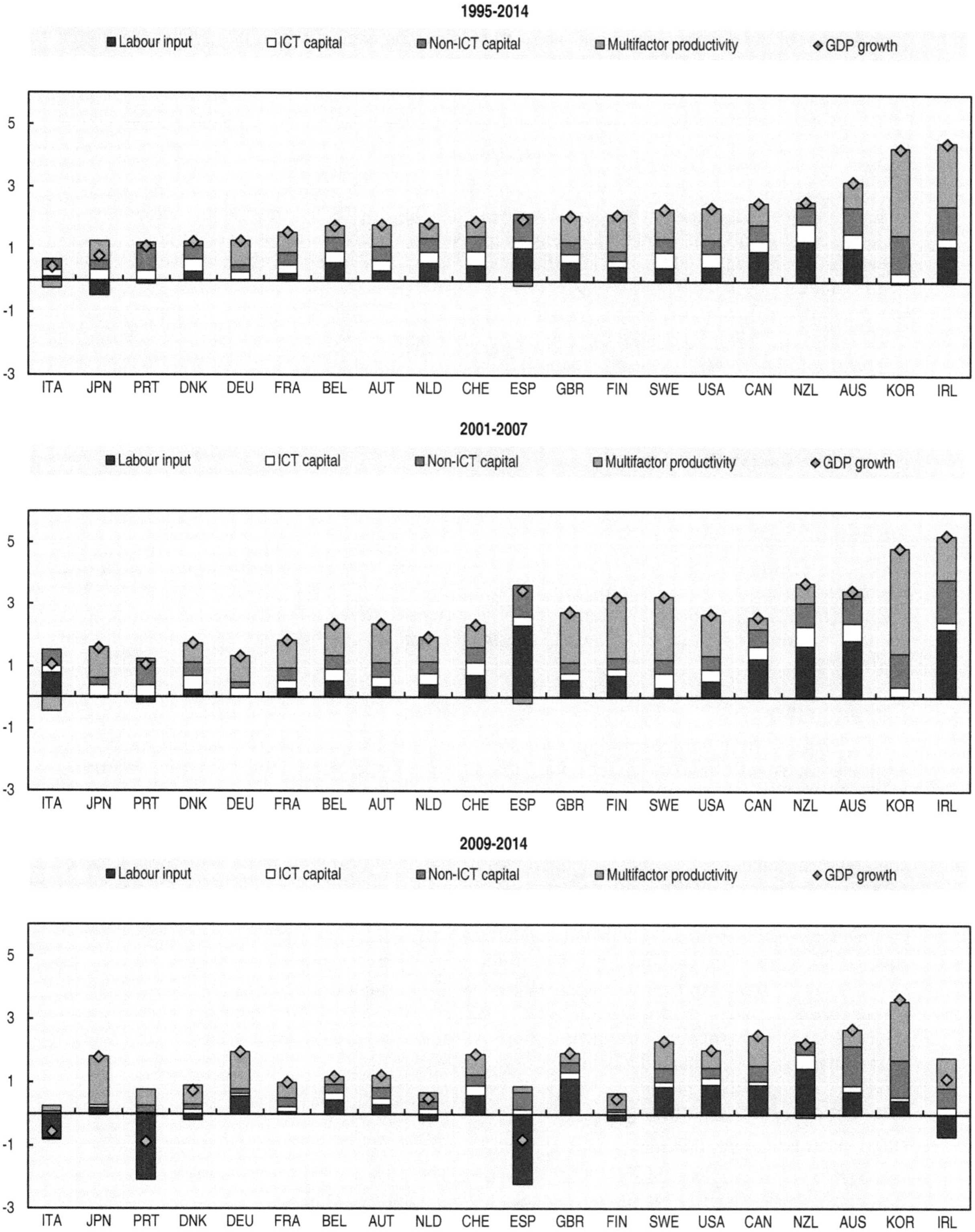

StatLink http://dx.doi.org/10.1787/888933346519

Multifactor productivity

Multifactor productivity (MFP) reflects the overall efficiency with which labour and capital inputs are used together in the production process. Labour productivity growth represents a higher level of output for every hour worked. This can be achieved if more capital per labour unit, i.e. capital deepening, is used in production, or by improving the overall efficiency with which labour and capital are used together, i.e. higher MFP.

Key facts

Over the past two decades, MFP growth varied considerably among OECD countries. Italy and Spain recorded the lowest (and negative) rates, lagging far behind the top performers Korea and Ireland. MFP growth decelerated in nearly all countries after the crisis compared with the period 2001-2007, with significant slowdowns in Finland, Sweden and the United Kingdom.

Large differences in MFP growth heavily affected labour productivity growth differentials. Prior to the crisis, relatively high MFP growth in most OECD countries contributed strongly to labour productivity growth, compared with the contributions of ICT and non-ICT capital deepening. In the post-crisis period, MFP appears to have moved pro-cyclically in most countries, as reflected by the slowdown in MFP growth and its much lower contribution to labour productivity growth, notably in Finland, Sweden, the United Kingdom and the United States.

Definition

By reformulating the growth accounting framework, labour productivity growth can be decomposed into the contribution of capital deepening and MFP. Capital deepening is defined as changes in the ratio of the total volume of capital services to total hours worked. Its contribution to labour productivity growth is calculated by weighting it with the share of capital costs in total costs (Annex A).

Comparability

Growth in MFP is measured as a residual, i.e. that part of GDP growth that cannot be explained by growth in labour and capital inputs. Traditionally, MFP growth is seen as capturing technological progress but, in practice, this interpretation needs some caution. Some part of technological change is embodied in capital input, e.g. improvements in design and quality between two vintages of the same capital asset, and so its effects on GDP growth are attributed to the respective factor. The measure of capital services in the *OECD Productivity Statistics* (database) takes explicit account of different productivities across assets, and price indices of ICT assets are adjusted for quality changes (Annexes A and C). Therefore, MFP only picks up disembodied technical change, e.g. network effects or spillovers from production factors, the effects of better management practices, brand names, organisational change and general knowledge.

Moreover, MFP also captures other factors such as adjustment costs, economies of scale, effects from imperfect competition and measurement errors. For instance, increases in educational attainment or a shift towards more skill-intensive production process, if not captured in the form of quality adjusted labour input – as is the case here – are captured by the MFP.

Sources and further reading

OECD, *OECD Productivity Statistics* (database), *http://dx.doi.org/10.1787/pdtvy-data-en.*

OECD (2001), *Measuring Productivity – OECD Manual, http://dx.doi.org/10.1787/9789264194519-en.*

Schreyer, P. (2004), "Capital Stocks, Capital Services and Multi-Factor Productivity Measures", *OECD Economic Studies*, Vol. 2003/2, *http://dx.doi.org/10.1787/eco_studies-v2003-art11-en.*

Wölfl, A. and D. Hajkova (2007), "Measuring Multifactor Productivity Growth", *OECD Science, Technology and Industry Working Papers*, No. 2007/05, *http://dx.doi.org/10.1787/246367010342.*

Figure 2.20. **Multifactor productivity growth**

Total economy, percentage change at annual rate

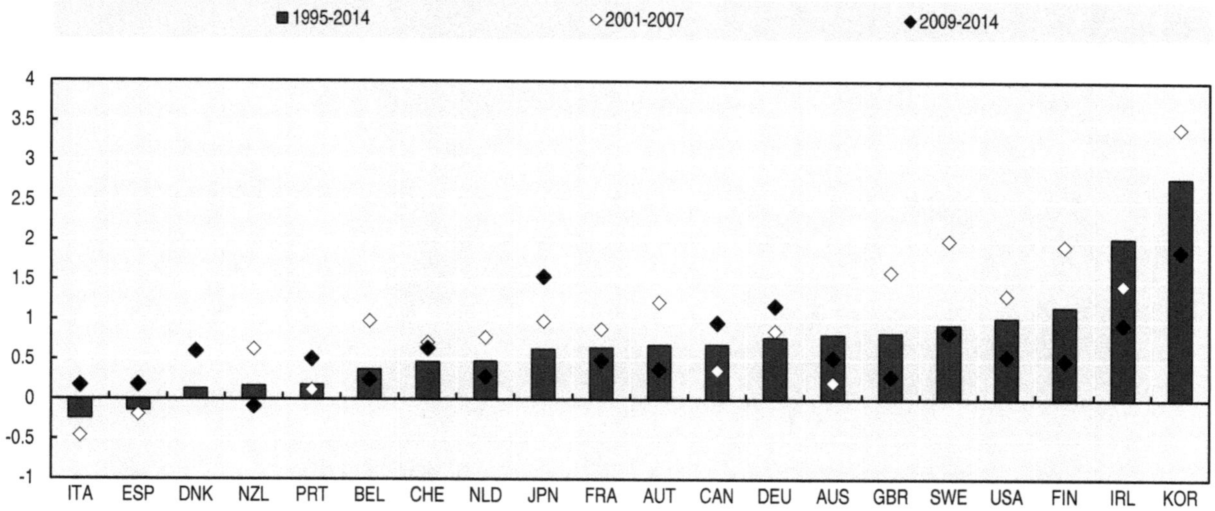

StatLink http://dx.doi.org/10.1787/888933346526

Figure 2.21. **Contributions to labour productivity growth**

Total economy, annual percentage point contribution

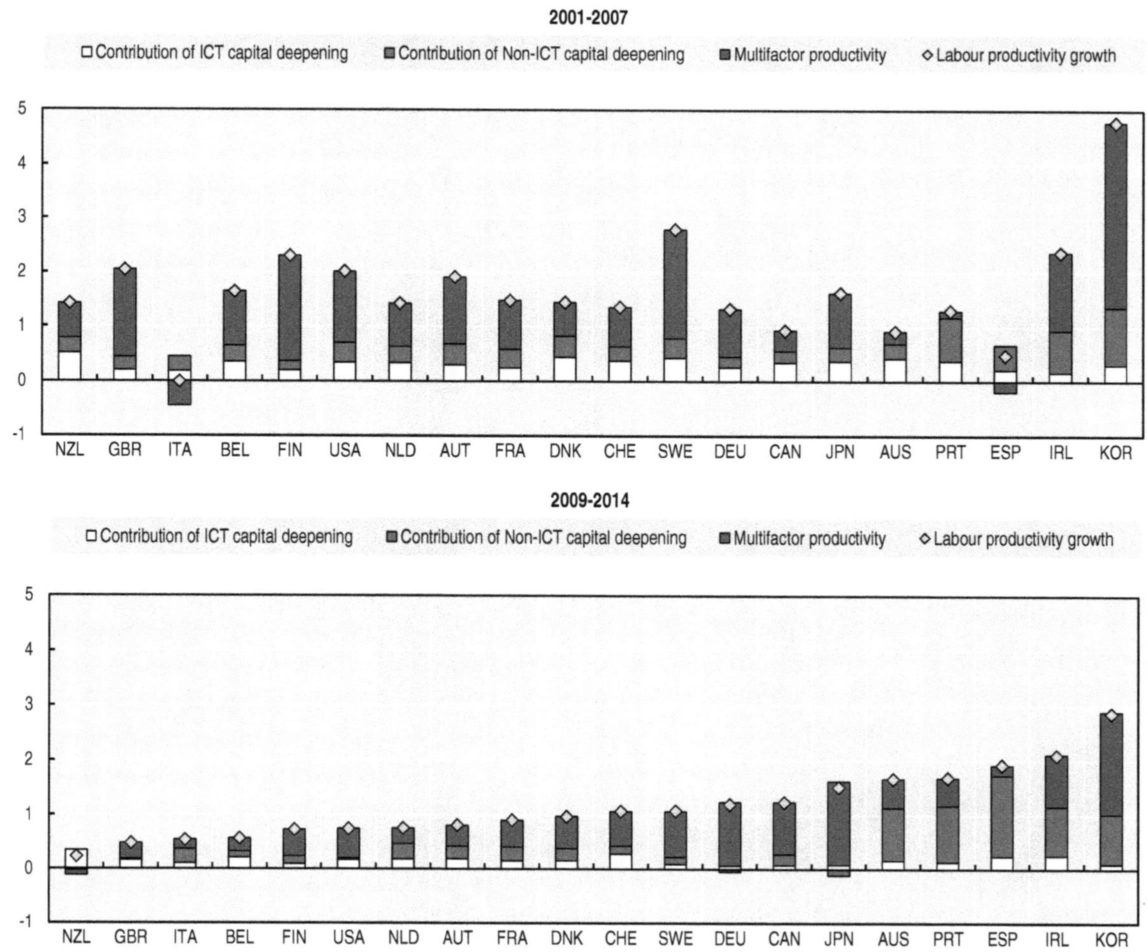

StatLink http://dx.doi.org/10.1787/888933346537

OECD Compendium of Productivity Indicators 2016

Chapter 3

Productivity by industry

Labour productivity by main economic activity

Sectors differ from each other with respect to their productivity growth. Such differences may relate, for instance, to the intensity with which sectors use skilled labour and physical and knowledge-based capital in their production, the scope for product and process innovation and the absorption of external knowledge, the degree of product standardisation, the scope for economies of scale, and the exposure to international competition through their participation in global value chains.

Key facts

Differences in productivity growth rates across countries are more evident when compared at the sectoral level. Although in most countries the highest growth rates are typically in the manufacturing sector and in some business sector services, productivity growth can differ considerably across countries. For instance, after the crisis between 2009 and 2014, productivity growth in manufacturing ranged from 0.3% in Greece to 8% in the Slovak Republic.

Compared with pre-crisis rates, labour productivity in manufacturing slowed in most OECD countries after the crisis, particularly in the Czech Republic, Finland and Korea. In business sector services, labour productivity also slowed after the crisis, notably in Estonia, Greece, Latvia and the United Kingdom.

Definition

Labour productivity is defined as real value added per hour worked. The non-agricultural business sector, excluding real estate, covers mining and quarrying; manufacturing; utilities; construction; and business sector services. The latter covers wholesale and retail trade, repair of motor vehicles and motor cycles; accommodation and food services; transportation and storage; information and communication services; financial and insurance activities; professional, scientific and support activities. This publication presents sectoral productivity growth for those countries for which sectoral data for real value added (in basic prices) and total hours worked by all persons employed (employees and self-employed) are available by ISIC Rev.4 breakdown in the *OECD National Accounts Statistics* (database).

Information on data for Israel: *http://dx.doi.org/10.1787/888932315602*.

Comparability

The comparability of productivity growth across industries and countries may be affected by problems in measuring real value added. This is particularly relevant for services, as measurement of price changes is complicated by difficulties in identifying quality changes and the provision of bundled services (Annex E). In some industries, estimates of real value added may be based on a sum-of-costs approach, which deflates, using some assumptions, compensation of employees in the specific sector. For example, most countries assume no change in labour productivity for public administration activities, which is why this industry is not included here. Real estate services are also excluded, as their value-added includes the imputation made for the dwelling services provided and consumed by home-owners.

Sources and further reading

Ahmad, N. et al. (2003), "Comparing Labour Productivity Growth in the OECD Area: The Role of Measurement", *OECD STI Working Paper*, No. 2003/14, *http://dx.doi.org/10.1787/126534183836*.

OECD Productivity Statistics (database), *http://dx.doi.org/10.1787/pdtvy-data-en*.

OECD National Accounts Statistics (database), *http://dx.doi.org/10.1787/na-data-en*.

OECD (2001), *Measuring Productivity – OECD Manual*, *http://dx.doi.org/10.1787/9789264194519-en*.

Wölfl, A. (2003), "Productivity Growth in Services Industries – An Assessment of Recent Patterns and the Role of Measurement", *OECD STI-Working Paper* 2003-7, *http://dx.doi.org/10.1787/086461104618*.

Figure 3.1. **Labour productivity by main activity**

Real value added per hour worked, percentage change at annual rate

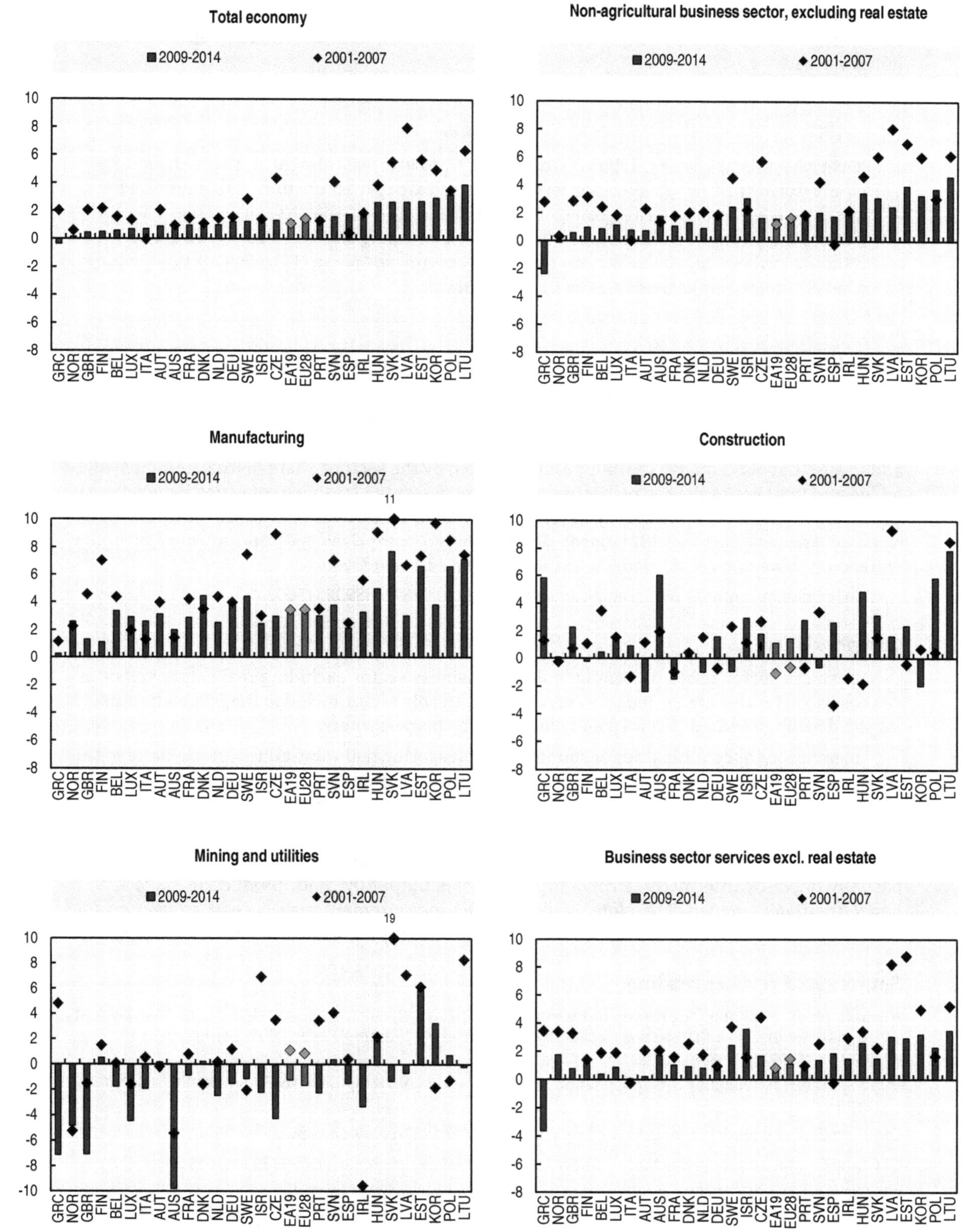

StatLink http://dx.doi.org/10.1787/888933346546

Industry contribution to business sector productivity

Understanding the drivers of productivity growth in the business sector requires an awareness of the contribution that each industry makes. The contribution of an individual sector depends not only on its productivity growth but also its share in total value added and hours worked.

Key facts

Over the past 15 years, labour productivity growth was almost entirely driven by manufacturing and business sector services. In the case of manufacturing, this reflects the typically higher productivity growth rates of the sector. In the case of business sector services, the strong contribution also reflects its increasing share in the overall economy. Excluding real estate, business sector services account for about 35 to 50% of total value added and total employment across OECD countries.

Definition

Labour productivity growth by industry is defined as the rate of change of real value added (in basic prices) per hour worked. The contribution of each sector to labour productivity growth of the total business sector is computed as the difference between the growth rate of value added and that of hours worked, with each weighted by the sector's share in total nominal value added and total hours worked respectively. Data are presented for those countries for which real value added and hours worked by sector are available by ISIC Rev.4 breakdown in the *OECD National Accounts Statistics* (database). Hours worked comprises the total number of hours worked by all persons employed, i.e. employees and self-employed.

Information on data for Israel: *http://dx.doi.org/10.1787/888932315602*.

Comparability

Business sector refers to non-agricultural business sector excluding real estate activities. Real estate activities are excluded as value-added in this sector includes the imputation made for the dwelling services provided and consumed by home-owners.

In addition to the difficulties encountered in measuring real value added, particularly in the services sector, it is also difficult to accurately measure nominal output in some cases. This is for example the case for the financial services sector, where some financial intermediation services, such as implicit banking charges, are indirectly measured.

Under- or over-estimation of the output of a particular sector, notably for services, will be partially offset by intermediate consumption of this output by other production sectors, and hence their value added. Therefore, while this mis-measurement may have an impact on the comparability across sectors, it may have a smaller impact on overall productivity growth.

Sources and further reading

Ahmad, N. et al. (2003), "Comparing Labour Productivity Growth in the OECD Area: The Role of Measurement", *OECD Science, Technology and Industry Working Paper* 2003-14, *http://dx.doi.org/10.1787/126534183836*.

Inter-Secretariat Working Group on National Accounts (ISWGNA), Task Force on FISIM (2013), *Final Report*.

OECD Productivity Statistics (database), *http://dx.doi.org/10.1787/pdtvy-data-en*.

OECD (2001), *Measuring Productivity – OECD Manual*, *http://dx.doi.org/10.1787/9789264194519-en*.

Pilat, D. and A. Wölfl (2005), "Measuring the Interaction between Manufacturing and Services", *OECD Science, Technology and Industry Working Paper* 2005-5, *http://dx.doi.org/10.1787/882376471514*.

Wölfl, A. (2003), "Productivity Growth in Services Industries – An Assessment of Recent Patterns and the Role of Measurement", *OECD Science, Technology and Industry – Working Paper* 2003-7, *http://dx.doi.org/10.1787/086461104618*.

Figure 3.2. **Industry contribution to business sector productivity growth**

Real value added per hour worked, percentage point contribution at annual rate

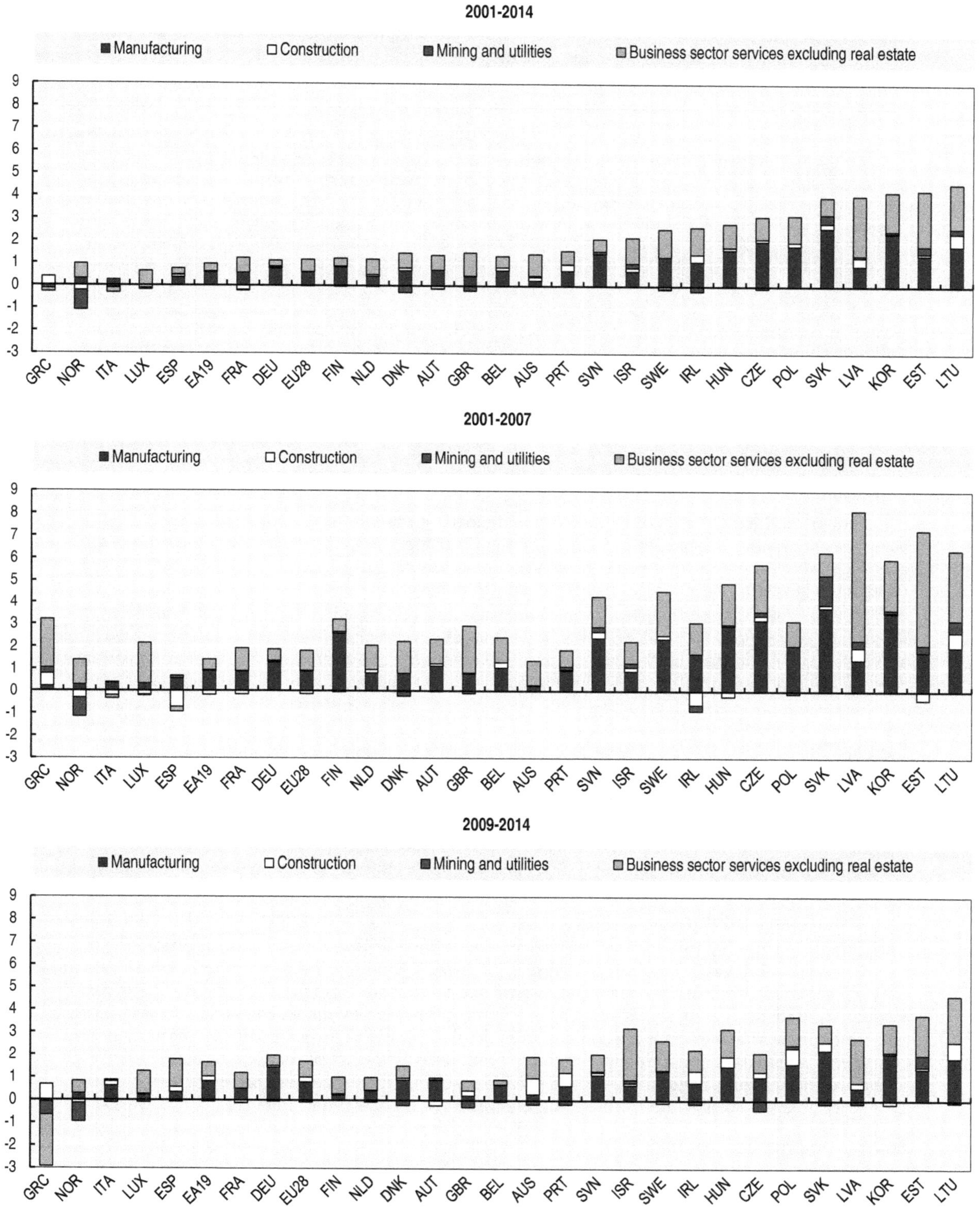

StatLink http://dx.doi.org/10.1787/888933346559

Labour productivity of business sector services

Developments in information and communication technologies (ICT) combined with internationally fragmented production processes are making business services increasingly dynamic, transportable and tradeable. As a result, several business sector services show characteristics similar to high-productivity manufacturing industries; they are intensive in ICT and knowledge-based capital, innovative, show economies of scale, and are increasingly exposed to international competition.

Key facts

Labour productivity growth varies substantially across business sector services. In the pre-crisis period, services that are traded internationally and thus with a higher exposure to international competition, such as information and communication services and finance and insurance activities, showed labour productivity growth rates that were as high as or even higher than those in the manufacturing sector. However, post the crisis, labour productivity growth in manufacturing was higher in most countries than in finance and insurance and information and communication services.

Labour productivity growth decelerated significantly in the finance sector, with negative growth rates in countries whose banking sectors were severely hit by the crisis, such as Greece, Ireland, Portugal, Spain and the United Kingdom. Productivity also slowed considerably in information and communication services, especially in Austria, Estonia, Greece, Latvia, Portugal and the Slovak Republic. Ireland on the other hand recorded the highest labour productivity growth in information and communication services, reflecting the presence of IT multinational headquarters producing high value added services.

Definition

Labour productivity growth by industry is defined as the rate of growth in real value added (in basic prices) per hour worked by industry. The figures present sectoral productivity growth for those countries which data on real value added and hours worked by sector are available by ISIC Rev. 4 breakdown in the *OECD National Accounts Statistics* (database).

The business sector services covers wholesale and retail trade, repair of motor vehicles and motorcycles, transportation and storage as well as accommodation and food services – presented here as "trade, hotels and transport"–; information and communication services; financial and insurance activities; and professional, scientific and support activities – reported here as "professional services".

Information on data for Israel: *http://dx.doi.org/10.1787/888932315602*.

Comparability

The comparability of productivity growth across industries and countries may be affected by problems in measuring real value added. This is particularly relevant for those business sector services where it is difficult to isolate price effects that are due to changes in the quality or in the mix of services provided as a bundle from pure price changes. Despite substantial progress made over the past 15 years in compiling service producer price indices (SPPIs), the methods used to compute constant price value added still vary across countries, affecting the measurement of productivity growth (Annex E).

Real estate activities are excluded from the business sector services, as their value-added includes the imputation made for the dwelling services provided and consumed by home-owners.

For some countries, labour force surveys (LFS) provide long time series for hours worked data at the total economy level, and hence for these countries, LFS data on hours worked are used in the *OECD Productivity Statistics* (database) for the whole economy. However, to ensure coherence across sectors, data on hours worked by sector are sourced from the *OECD National Accounts Statistics* (database). This can affect comparability of productivity growth by industry with that of the total economy presented in the previous chapter. In addition, certain services sectors are characterised by a high degree of part-time work and self-employment, which can affect the quality of estimates of actual hours worked.

Sources and further reading

OECD Productivity Statistics (database), *http://dx.doi.org/10.1787/pdtvy-data-en*.

Pilat, D. and A. Wölfl (2005), "Measuring the Interaction between Manufacturing and Services", *OECD Science, Technology and Industry Working Paper* 2005-5, *http://dx.doi.org/10.1787/882376471514*.

Wölfl, A. (2005), "The Service Economy in OECD Countries", *OECD Science, Technology and Industry – Working Paper* 2005-3, *http://dx.doi.org/10.1787/212257000720*.

Wölfl, A. (2003), "Productivity Growth in Services Industries – An Assessment of Recent Patterns and the Role of Measurement", *OECD Science, Technology and Industry – Working Paper* 2003-7, *http://dx.doi.org/10.1787/086461104618*.

Figure 3.3. **Labour productivity by business sector services**

Real value added per hour worked, percentage change at annual rate

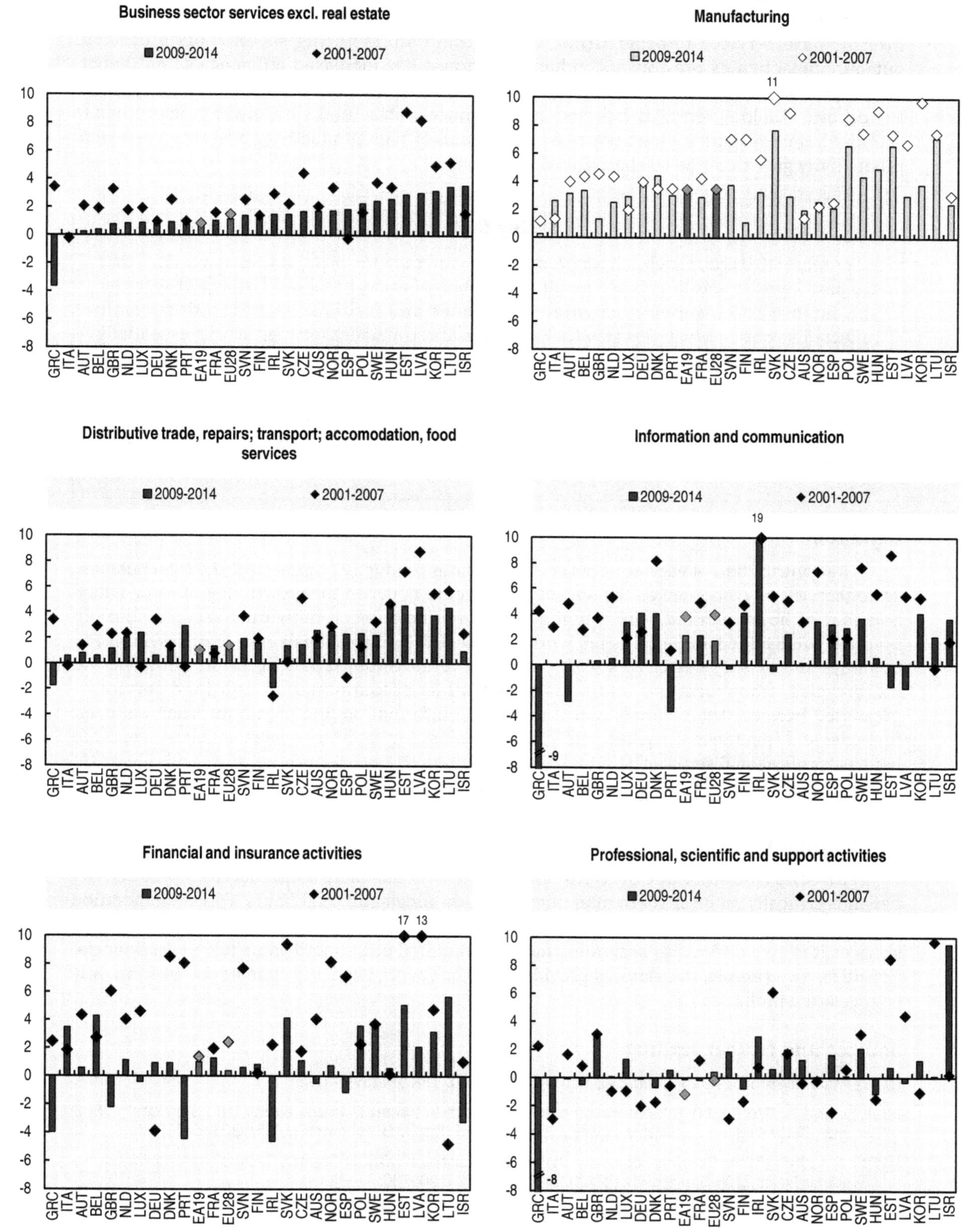

StatLink http://dx.doi.org/10.1787/888933346560

Contributions to business sector services' productivity

The business services sector has contributed significantly to GDP growth across OECD countries in recent decades, driven by an increase in the number of firms providing intermediate services to other firms, also in the manufacturing sector. This process of outsourcing activities previously conducted in-house has increased efficiencies, and hence, labour productivity, of both outsourcing firms as well as the specialised intermediary firms. Hence, over the long term, both factors may produce a structural shift towards intermediate services industries and a direct positive contribution of high productivity business services to productivity growth of the total economy.

Key facts

For most OECD countries, labour productivity growth in the business sector services over the past 15 years was largely the result of distributive trade, hotels and transport services, and finance and insurance activities. For finance and insurance services, this mainly reflected strong productivity growth. For hotels and transport services, it was essentially due to their large shares in total business sector services value added and hours worked.

However, after the crisis, in most OECD economies, labour productivity growth was mainly accounted for by trade, hotels and transport; and information and communication, with finance and insurance services which were deeply affected by the global financial crisis making a smaller contribution.

Definition

The contribution of each services sector to labour productivity growth of the total business sector services is computed as the weighted difference between the growth rate of value added and that of hours worked. The weights are computed as each individual sector's share in nominal value added and total hours worked respectively of total business sector services. The business sector services covers wholesale and retail trade, repair of motor vehicles and motorcycles, transportation and storage as well as accommodation and food services – presented here as "trade, hotels and transport" –; information and communication services; financial and insurance activities; and professional, scientific and support activities -reported here as "professional services".

Information on data for Israel: *http://dx.doi.org/10.1787/888932315602*.

Comparability

The contribution of one services industry to total business sector services productivity depends critically on its share in total nominal value added and total hours worked. In addition to the difficulties encountered in measuring price changes in the services sector, for some services it is also difficult to accurately measure nominal output and value added. In financial activities, for example, the services provided are not always explicitly charged for and can only be measured indirectly.

Sources and further reading

OECD Productivity Statistics (database), *http://dx.doi.org/10.1787/pdtvy-data-en*.

Pilat, D. and A. Wölfl (2005), "Measuring the Interaction between Manufacturing and Services", *OECD Science, Technology and Industry Working Paper* 2005-5, *http://dx.doi.org/10.1787/882376471514*.

Wölfl, A. (2005), "The Service Economy in OECD Countries", *OECD Science, Technology and Industry – Working Paper* 2005-3, *http://dx.doi.org/10.1787/212257000720*.

Wölfl, A. (2003), "Productivity Growth in Services Industries – An Assessment of Recent Patterns and the Role of Measurement", *OECD Science, Technology and Industry – Working Paper* 2003-7, *http://dx.doi.org/10.1787/086461104618*.

Figure 3.4. **Contributions to productivity growth of business sector services**

Real value added per hour worked, percentage point contribution at annual rate

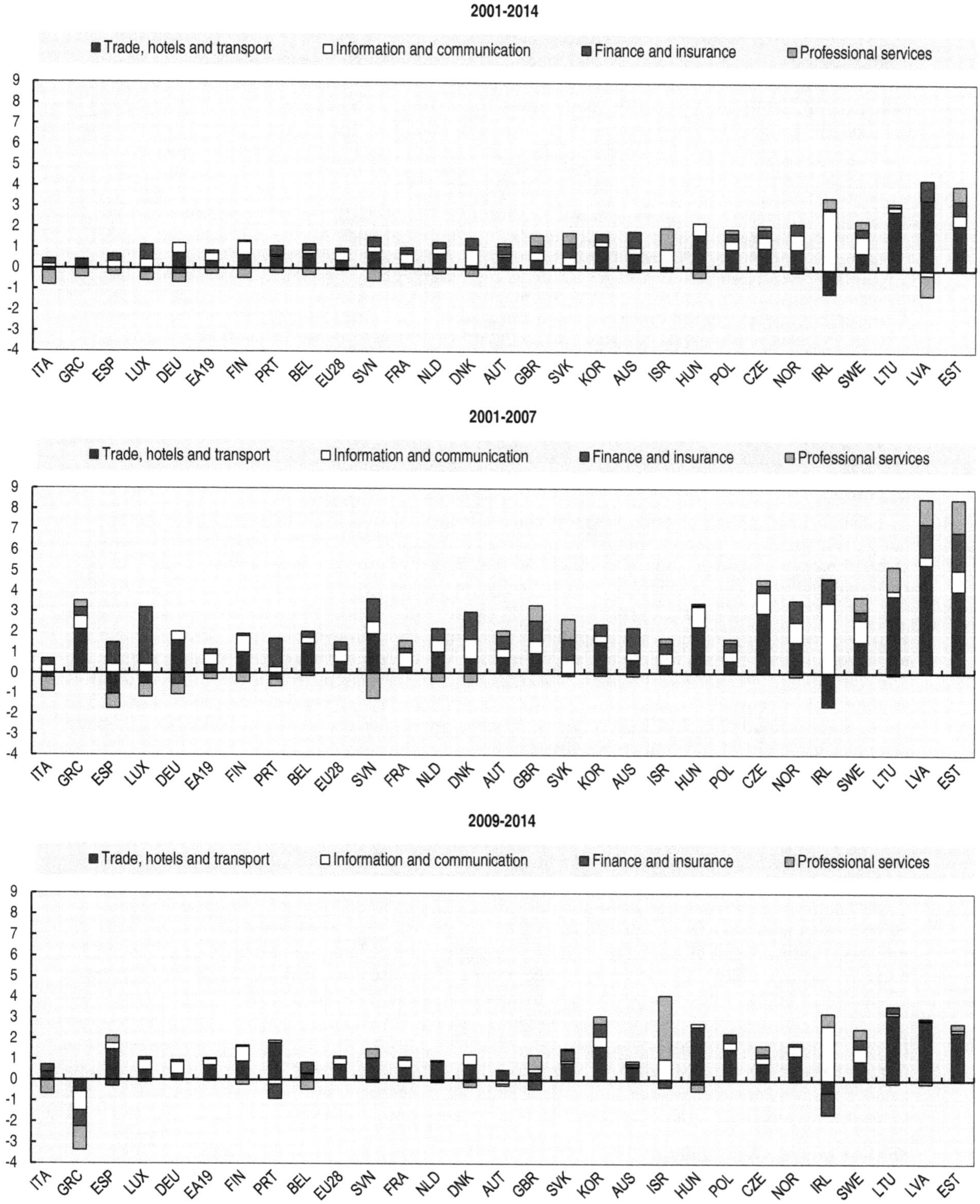

StatLink http://dx.doi.org/10.1787/888933346571

Productivity by enterprise size

Firm heterogeneity and business dynamism matter for productivity. Productivity tends to increase with firm size, as large firms exploit increasing returns to scale. However, new small firms are often found to spur aggregate productivity growth as they enter with new technologies and stimulate productivity-enhancing changes by incumbents. The reallocation of resources across enterprises, driven by firm dynamics, is also expected to increase aggregate productivity via a process of "creative destruction", whereby innovative firms enter the market and expand while displacing lower productivity firms.

Key facts

Larger firms are on average more productive than smaller ones, particularly in the manufacturing sector, partly reflecting increasing returns to scale, for instance, through capital intensive production. But smaller firms can outperform larger, particularly in the services sector, pointing to competitive advantages in niche, high brand or high intellectual property content activities as well as the intensive use of affordable ICT. In most countries, labour productivity gaps between micro and, to a lower extent small and medium-sized firms, and large firms are relatively high. In Ireland, average labour productivity of large manufacturing firms is significantly higher compared with other countries, reflecting in large part the high intellectual property content of their output, typically provided by foreign parents.

Labour productivity growth tends to be higher in countries with higher start-up rates and churn rates, reflecting the role of new firms in driving aggregate productivity growth.

Definition

Labour productivity by enterprise size class is measured as gross value added in current prices per person employed. Labour input is measured as total employment, which includes employees and all other paid or unpaid persons who worked for the concerned unit during the reference year. Data on hours worked by all persons employed are typically not available by industry and enterprise size class.

Churn rates reflect a country's degree of creative destruction and business dynamism. The employer enterprise churn rate is computed as the sum of the employer enterprise birth rate and the employer enterprise death rate, following the *Eurostat-OECD Manual on Business Demography Statistics*. The start-up rate is defined as the share of 0-2 year-old firms in the total firm population. The services sector covers: wholesale and retail trade, repair of motor vehicles and motorcycles; transportation and storage; accommodation and food services; information and communication services; real estate activities; professional and support activities.

Comparability

Value added estimates for different enterprise size classes are based on *OECD Structural and Demographic Business Statistics* (database) and will typically not align with estimates in national accounts. The latter include a number of adjustments to reflect businesses and activities that may not be covered in structural business statistics, such as those made to reflect the Non-Observed Economy. Since labour input is measured as total employment, comparability of labour productivity measures by size class may be affected by differences in the share of part-time employment. In addition, productivity differences in main aggregate sectors could mask different productivity patterns in more narrowly defined industries. This may in turn reflect differences in the value of goods and services produced, as well as different intensities in the use of knowledge-based capital.

For all countries measures of birth and death rates are in line with the Eurostat-OECD Manual. Large countries are, other things equal, likely to exhibit lower birth rates than smaller countries as firms are able to expand within the national economic territory via the creation of new establishments. For smaller countries similar events will be recorded as a birth if the parent enterprise in one country expands by the creation of an affiliate enterprise in a neighbouring country.

Sources and further reading

OECD Productivity Statistics (database), *http://dx.doi.org/10.1787/pdtvy-data-en*.

OECD Structural and Demographic Business Statistics (database), *http://dx.doi.org/10.1787/sdbs-data-en*.

OECD/Eurostat (2008), *Eurostat-OECD Manual on Business Demography Statistics*, OECD Publishing, Paris, *http://dx.doi.org/10.1787/9789264041882-en*.

OECD (2015), *Entrepreneurship at a Glance 2015*, OECD Publishing, Paris, *http://dx.doi.org/10.1787/entrepreneur_aag-2015-en*.

Figure 3.5. **Labour productivity by firm size, manufacturing**

Value added per person employed, large firms (250 workers or more) = 100

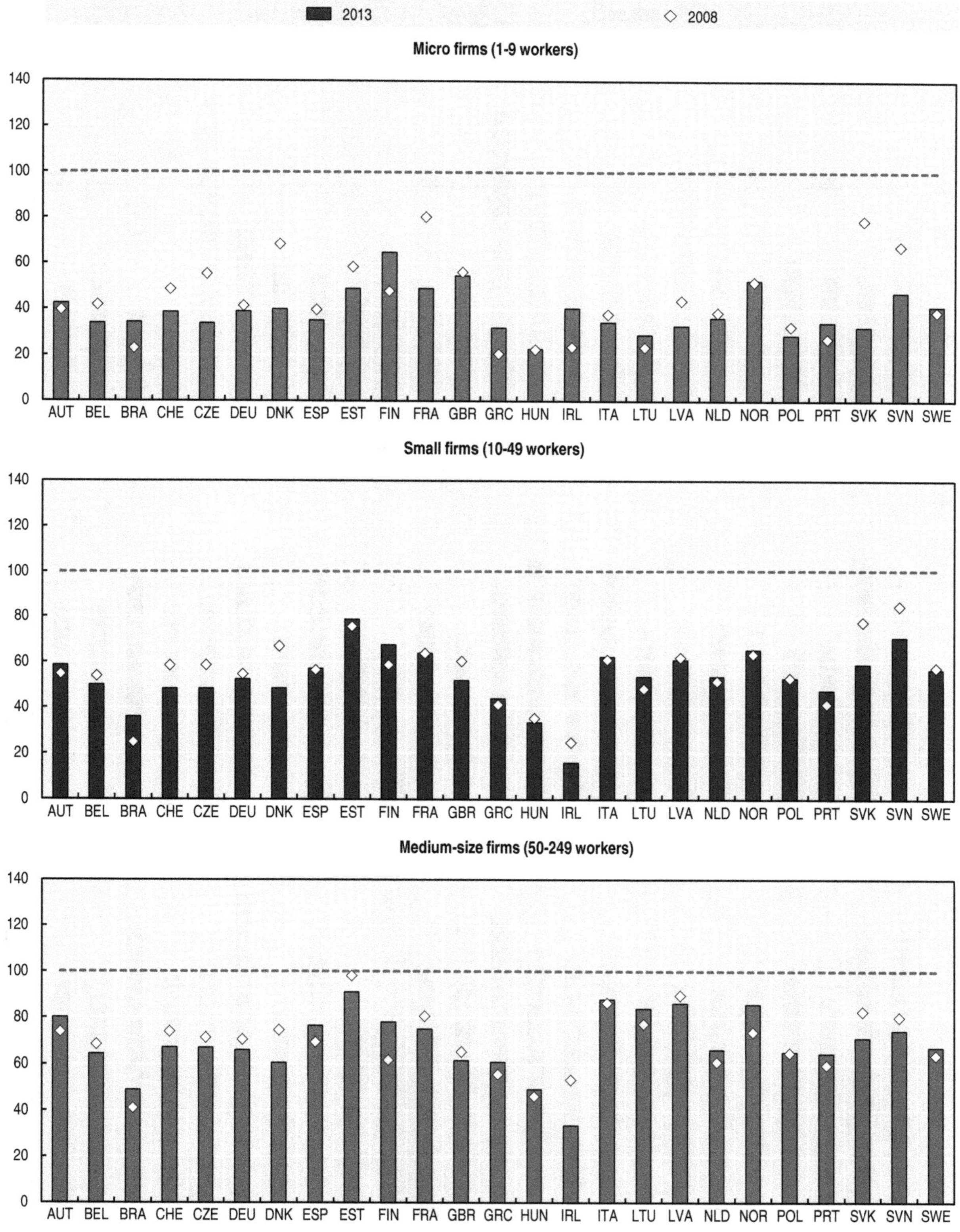

StatLink http://dx.doi.org/10.1787/888933346587

Figure 3.6. **Labour productivity by firm size, services**

Value added per person employed, large firms (250 workers or more) = 100

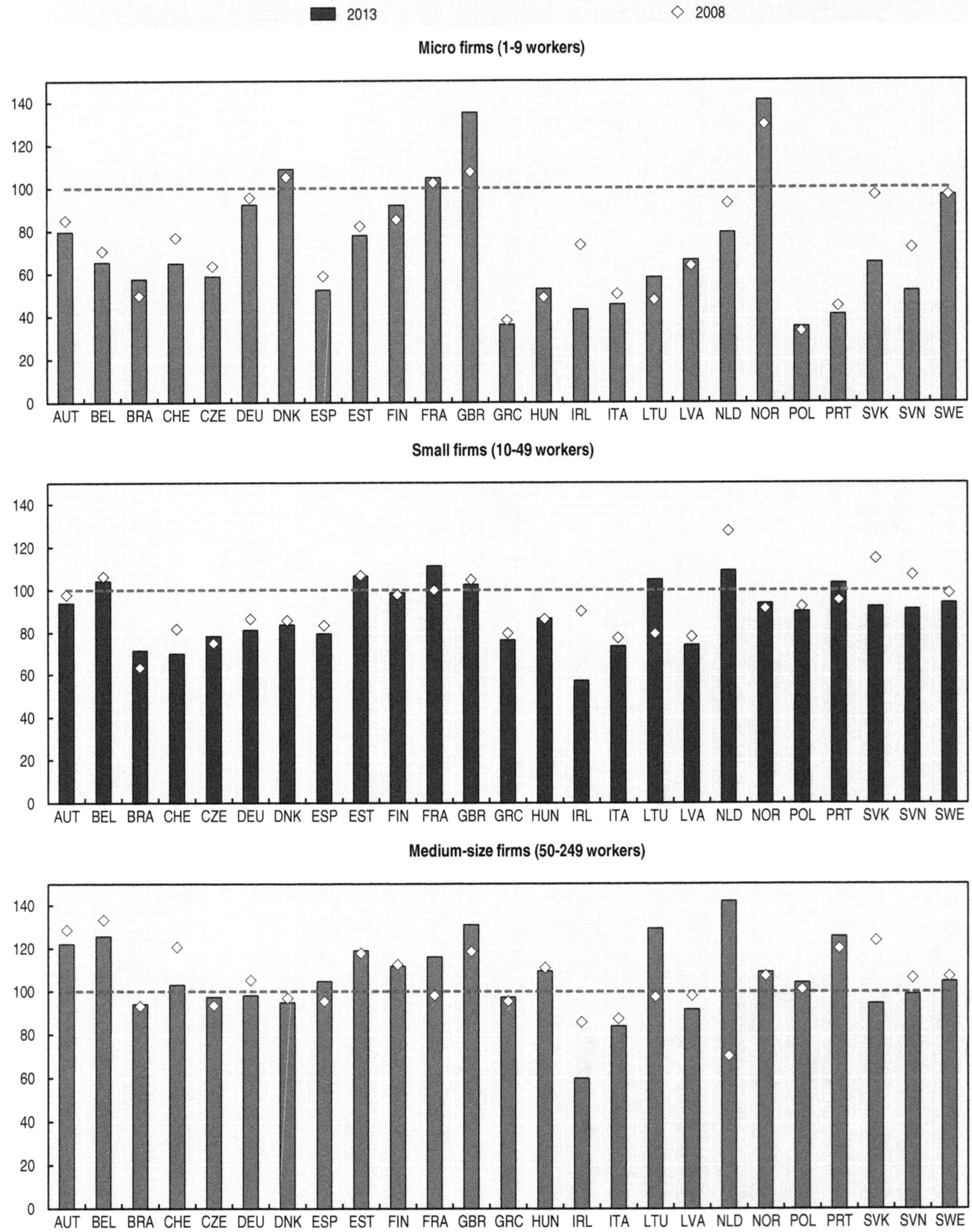

StatLink http://dx.doi.org/10.1787/888933346593

Figure 3.7. **Start-up rates and labour productivity growth**

Percentage of total firm population (x-axis); average annual growth of gross value added per hour worked (y-axis)

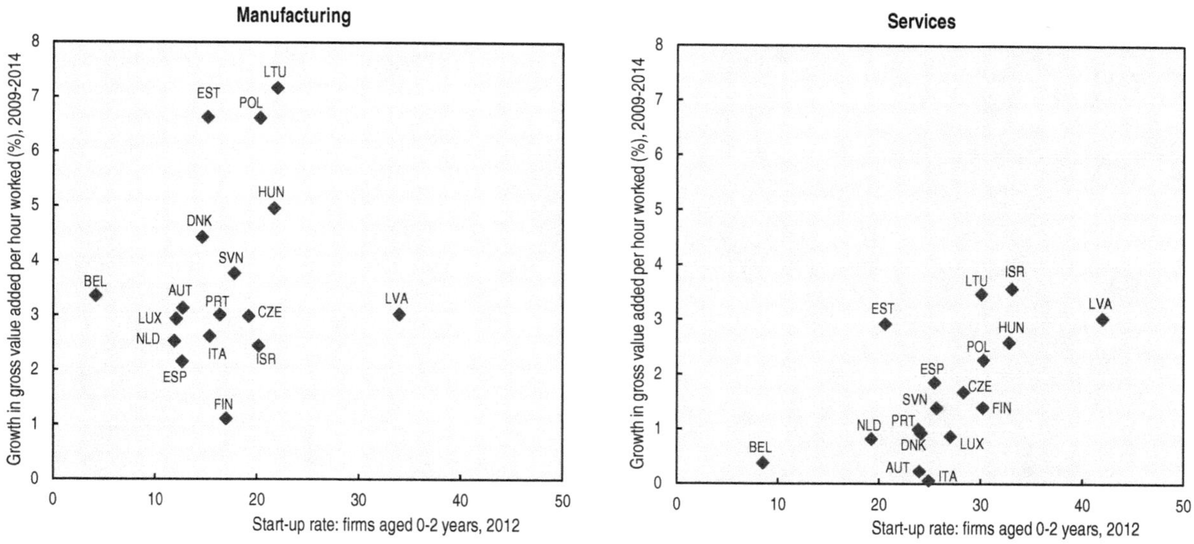

StatLink http://dx.doi.org/10.1787/888933346607

Figure 3.8. **Churn rates and labour productivity growth**

Churn rates (x-axis); average annual growth in gross value added per hour worked (y-axis)

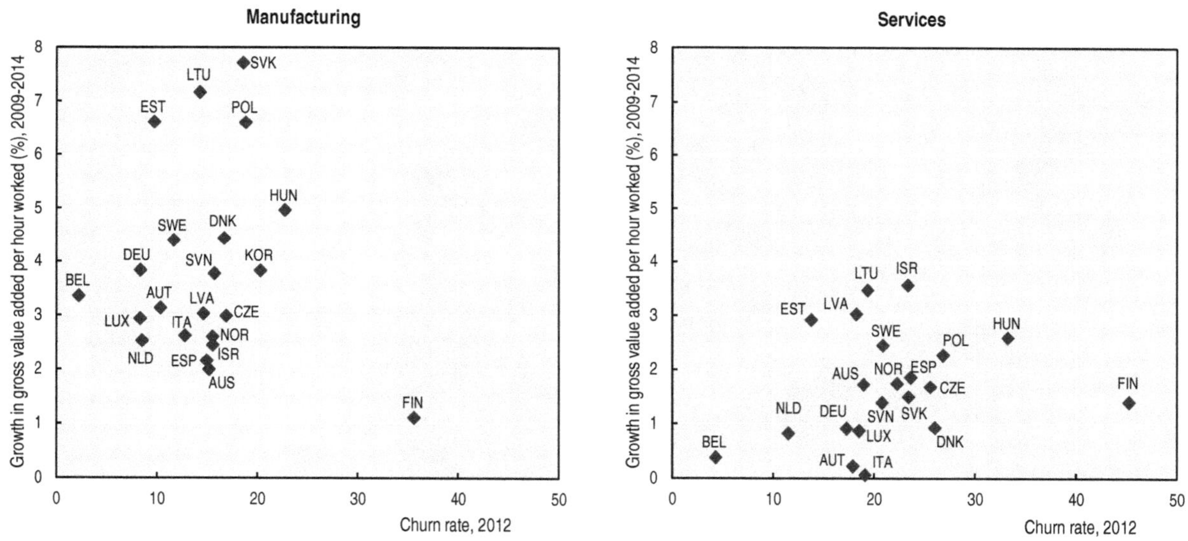

StatLink http://dx.doi.org/10.1787/888933346616

OECD Compendium of Productivity Indicators 2016

Chapter 4

Productivity, trade and international competitiveness

Unit labour costs

International competitiveness

The importance of global value chains

Unit labour costs

Unit labour costs (ULCs) reflect total labour costs relative to a volume of output. Hence, the growth in unit labour costs is often viewed as a broad measure of (international) price competitiveness of firms within a country.

Key facts

Over the last 15 years, many OECD countries improved their competitiveness relative to others by keeping ULCs in check in both manufacturing and business sector services, as was the case of Germany, Ireland, Israel and Poland. In these countries, low increases in ULCs reflected relatively strong labour productivity growth and/or moderate wage increases. In other countries, such as Lithuania, the Slovak Republic and Slovenia, large productivity gains contributed to keep ULCs in check in the manufacturing sector while wage inflation, in particular, in business sector services, led to substantial increases in ULCs.

Within Europe, Greece, Ireland, Portugal and Spain, saw strong falls in their ULC since the onset of the financial crisis. However, care is needed in interpreting these results as improved relative competiveness, as they need to be balanced against the significant falls in output and labour input seen during that period. In Germany, improvements in competitiveness prior to the crisis show signs of being reversed in recent years.

Definition

ULCs are defined as the average cost of labour per unit of output produced. They can be expressed as the ratio of total labour compensation per hour worked to output per hour worked (labour productivity). Compensation of employees is defined as the total remuneration payable by an enterprise to an employee in return for work done by the latter during the accounting period. It includes wages and salaries payable in cash or in kind, as well as social insurance contributions paid by employers. Total labour compensation is for total persons employed and so includes employees and the self-employed.

Information on data for Israel: *http://dx.doi.org/10.1787/888932315602*.

Comparability

The data are presented for the total economy, manufacturing and business sector services (which exclude real estate activities) according to the ISIC Rev. 4 classification. All the ULC components are sourced from the *OECD National Accounts Statistics* (database), respectively the *OECD Productivity Statistics* (database). The figures present the data for those countries for which time series of sectoral hours worked are available in the *OECD National Accounts Statistics* (database).

Manufacturing ULCs are often perceived as more representative for assessing competition in tradable products. Services prices are often not very reliable, which may affect the cross-country comparability of measured business sector services ULC.

Sources/online databases

OECD National Accounts Statistics (database), *http://dx.doi.org/10.1787/na-data-en*.

OECD Productivity Statistics (database), *http://dx.doi.org/10.1787/pdtvy-data-en*.

Figure 4.1. **Unit labour costs, hourly labour compensation and productivity, total economy**

Percentage change at annual rate

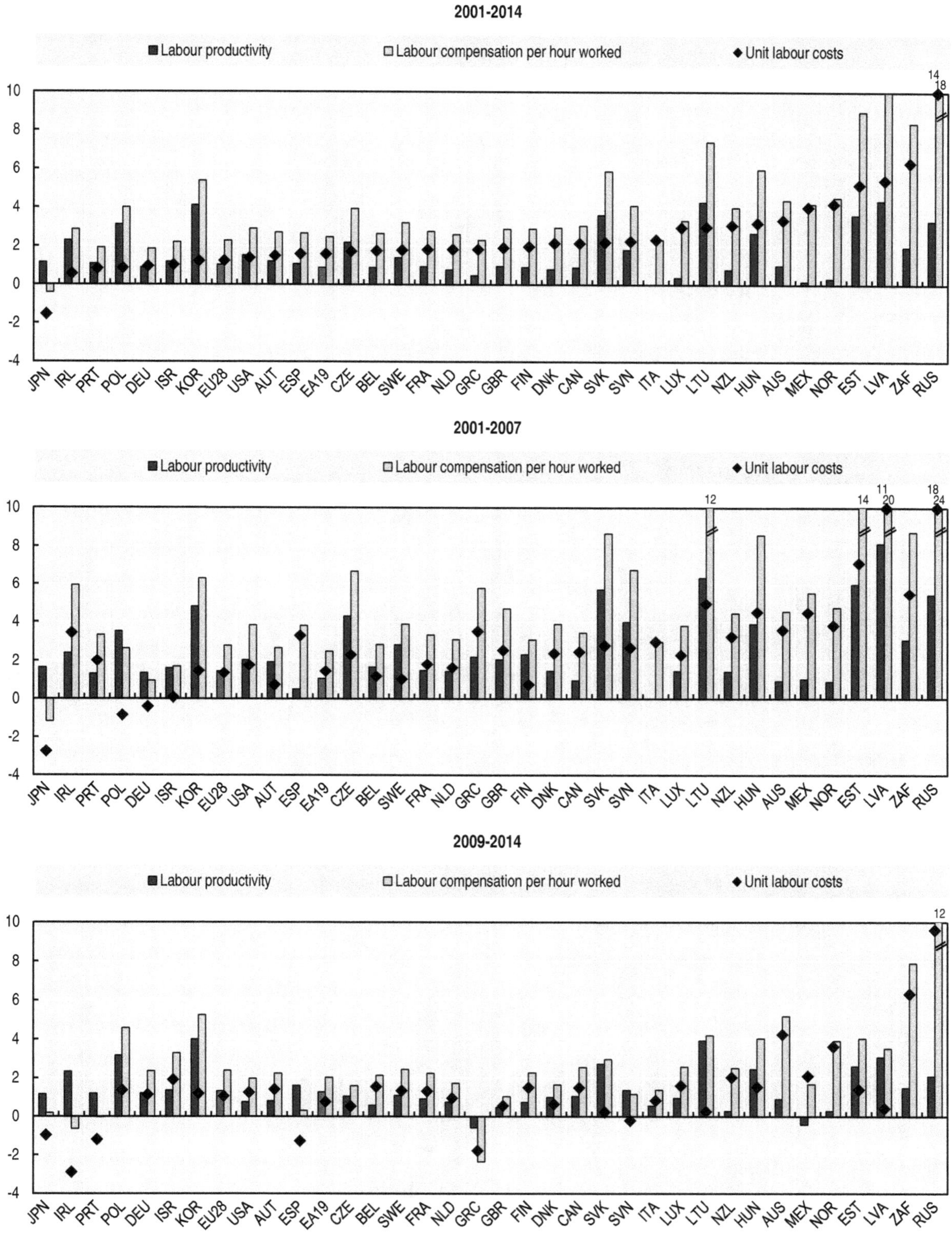

StatLink http://dx.doi.org/10.1787/888933346625

Figure 4.2. **Unit labour costs, hourly labour compensation and productivity, manufacturing**

Percentage change at annual rate

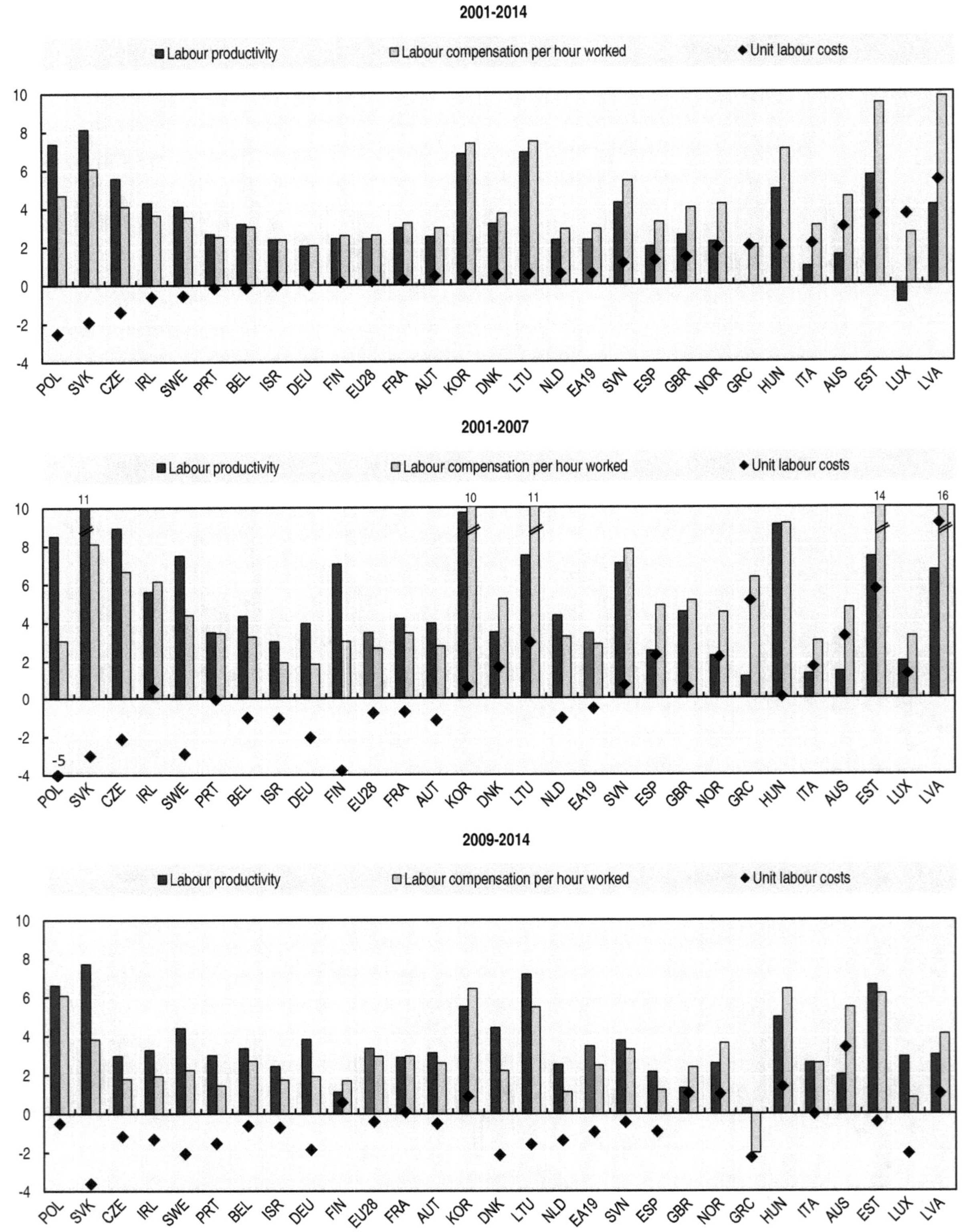

StatLink http://dx.doi.org/10.1787/888933346633

Figure 4.3. **Unit labour costs, hourly labour compensation and productivity, business sector services**

Percentage change at annual rate

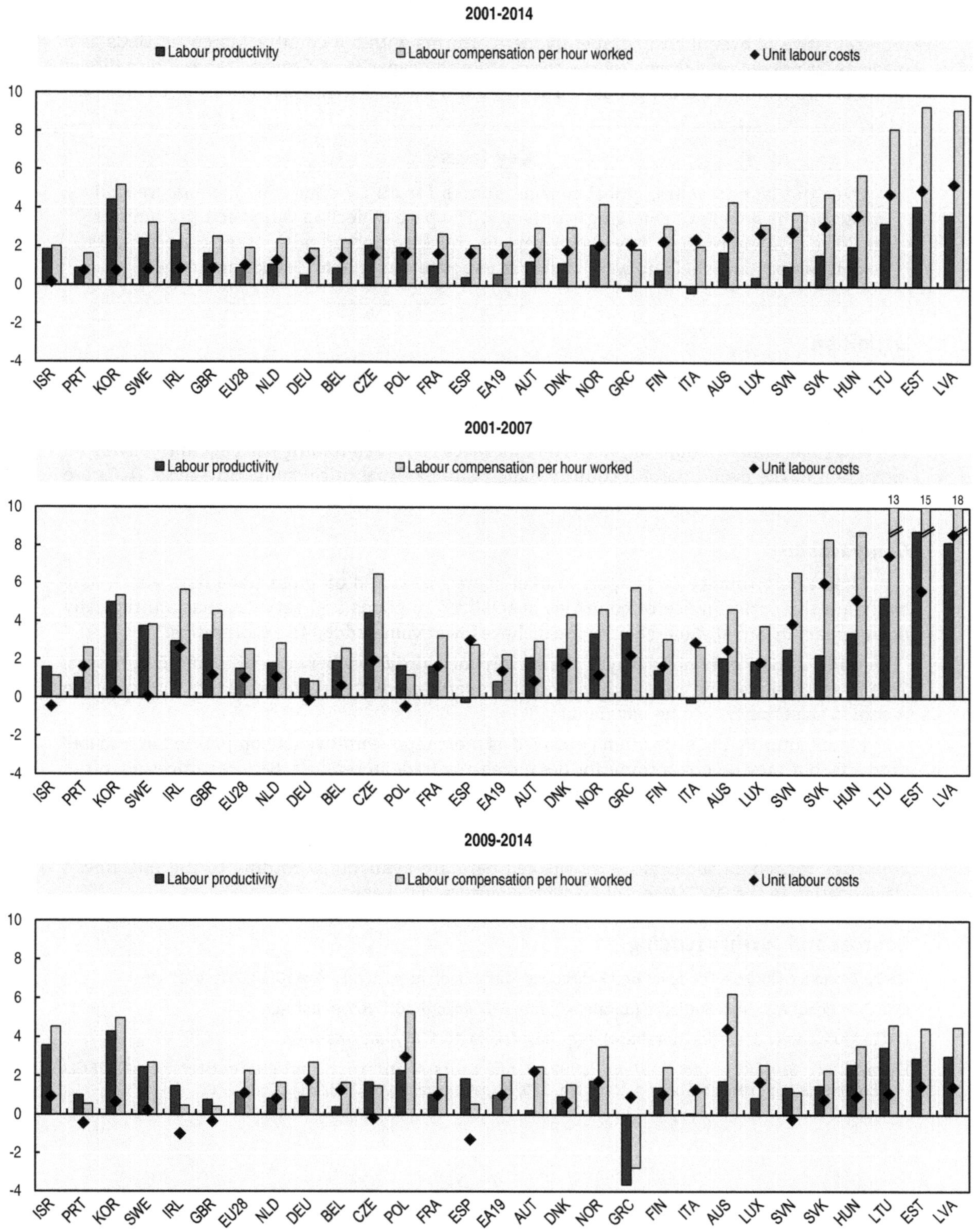

StatLink http://dx.doi.org/10.1787/888933346646

International competitiveness

Despite their frequent use, unit labour costs (ULCs) are an incomplete measure of international competitiveness and they need to be complemented with other indicators. In an era of global value chains, a measure based only on the costs of domestic labour may not be representative of overall cost competitiveness of firms within a country. Moreover, ULCs as a measure of price-competitiveness cannot capture the capacity of firms to serve international markets through high quality goods and services and where demand is relatively price inelastic.

Key facts

Over the last 15 years, global market shares for all G7 countries have decreased, reflecting the growth of emerging economies. The pace of decline varied across countries. In Germany, where ULCs have been kept in check compared with other countries, its export performance held up well, while the opposite was true for France and Italy.

Definition

Export performance is measured as actual growth in exports relative to the growth of the country's export market. The export market share for a single country measures the share of exports by firms in that country in relation to world exports of all countries. Real effective exchange rates take account of price level differences between trading partners and provide an indication of the evolution of a country's aggregate external price competitiveness. ULCs are defined as the average cost of labour per unit of output produced.

Comparability

Export performance and export market shares are based on gross trade data which may overstate the performance of countries specialised in goods and services that are typically downstream in global value-chains, and so have lower value-added to export ratios.

Trade statistics do not always consistently measure flows between affiliated enterprises. This is especially so for trade in intellectual property products where payments may often be recorded as property income payments.

Manufacturing ULCs are often perceived as more representative for competition in tradable products, but they do not account for the increasing trade in services. Services prices are often not very reliable, and therefore may affect cross-country comparability of ULCs in the business sector services. Looking at total economy ULCs somewhat alleviates these concerns, but their coverage goes significantly beyond the tradable sector. ULC data are only presented for those countries for which sectoral hours worked data are available according to the ISIC Rev. 4 classification in the *OECD National Accounts (Statistics)* database.

Sources and further reading

OECD Economic Outlook: Statistics and Projections (database), *http://dx.doi.org/10.1787/eo-data-en.*

OECD National Accounts Statistics (database), *http://dx.doi.org/10.1787/na-data-en.*

OECD Productivity Statistics (database), *http://dx.doi.org/10.1787/pdtvy-data-en.*

Durand, M., Simon, J. and C. Webb (1992), "Indicators of international competitiveness", *OECD Economics Department Working Paper* No. 120, *http://dx.doi.org/10.1787/708306180711.*

Figure 4.4. **Indicators of international competitiveness**

Indices, 2001 = 100

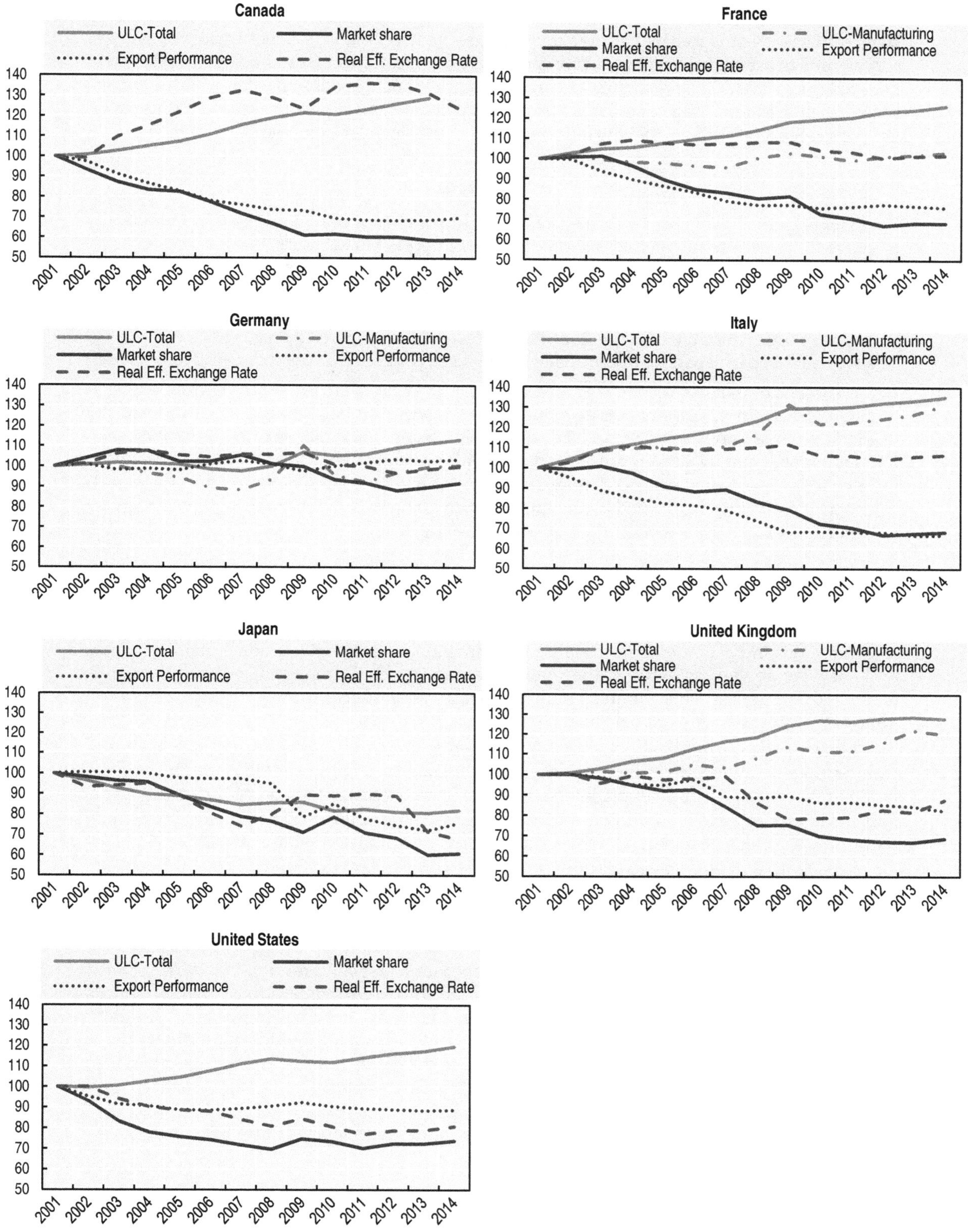

StatLink http://dx.doi.org/10.1787/888933346658

The importance of global value chains

Economic theory suggests that more open countries should grow faster and have higher income levels than less open ones. International trade enables firms to specialise in goods and services that can be most efficiently produced in the home country; to sell to larger markets, hence exploiting economies of scale; and to benefit from higher quality and variety of inputs as well as technological spillovers and knowledge exchange. Trade also puts pressure on prices for final goods and intermediate inputs and facilitates international fragmentation of production processes, further reducing costs. Firms exposed to international competition ought to innovate continuously in order to succeed.

Key facts

The empirical evidence confirms the strong link between trade and growth. More open countries, where trade openness is measured by imports plus exports as a per cent of GDP, typically have a higher level of GDP per capita. Moreover, with the exception of the Russian Federation, countries that have been able to increase their exports-to-GDP ratio over time have also improved labour productivity over the same period. This is particularly the case for catch-up economies such as the Central and Eastern European countries and Korea, which suggests that participation in global value chains has contributed to the catching-up process.

Measures of exports based on gross terms can however overstate the importance that a given growth in exports makes to overall GDP growth; this reflects the fact that exports increasingly embody imports. Indeed, the foreign value added share of gross exports has augmented in nearly all countries over the past fifteen years, reflecting growing participation into GVCs. This has amplified the opportunities for higher specialisation, and so increased export driven growth reflected by the higher ratios of direct domestic value content of gross exports to GDP, possibly contributing to productivity gains.

Definition

Typically, international trade statistics measure trade on a gross basis as net exports, i.e. exports minus imports. Exports on a gross basis include the value of imports embodied in goods and services as well as some value-added created in other domestic sectors that returns embodied in imports. This "double-counting" particularly affects those countries where firms are closely integrated into global value chains.

Measuring international trade in value-added terms attempts to correct for the double-counting. Value-added embodied in foreign final demand – as represented in the bottom right panel of Figure 4.5 – can most readily be interpreted as "exports of value-added". It shows how industries export value added that is produced in the home country to foreign final consumers, both through direct final exports and via indirect exports of intermediate inputs.

Information on data for Israel: *http://dx.doi.org/10.1787/888932315602*.

Comparability

The indicators in the joint *OECD/WTO Statistics on Trade in Value Added (TiVA)* (database) are derived from OECD Input Output Tables linked together using bilateral trade flows in goods and services. Some assumptions are necessary to create the TiVA indicators, implying that some care is needed in interpreting the results. Key in this context is the underlying "production assumption" that assumes that for a given industry, all firms allocated to that industry use the same goods and services, and so imports, to produce the same outputs. Firms engaged in global value chains, particularly foreign owned affiliates, are likely to have higher import content than firms in the same sector producing goods or services for domestic markets. This means that TiVA estimates will, more likely than not, underestimate the import content of exports.

Sources and further reading

OECD National Accounts Statistics (database), *http://dx.doi.org/10.1787/na-data-en*.

OECD-WTO: *Statistics on Trade in Value Added* (database), *http://dx.doi.org/10.1787/data-00648-en*.

OECD-WTO (2012), "Trade in Value Added: Concepts, Methodologies and Challenges" (OECD-WTO, online document), *www.oecd.org/sti/ind/49894138.pdf*.

Figure 4.5. **Trade openness and GDP per capita vis-à-vis the OECD, 2014**

Total economy, percentage differences vis-à-vis the OECD average, in current prices and current PPPs

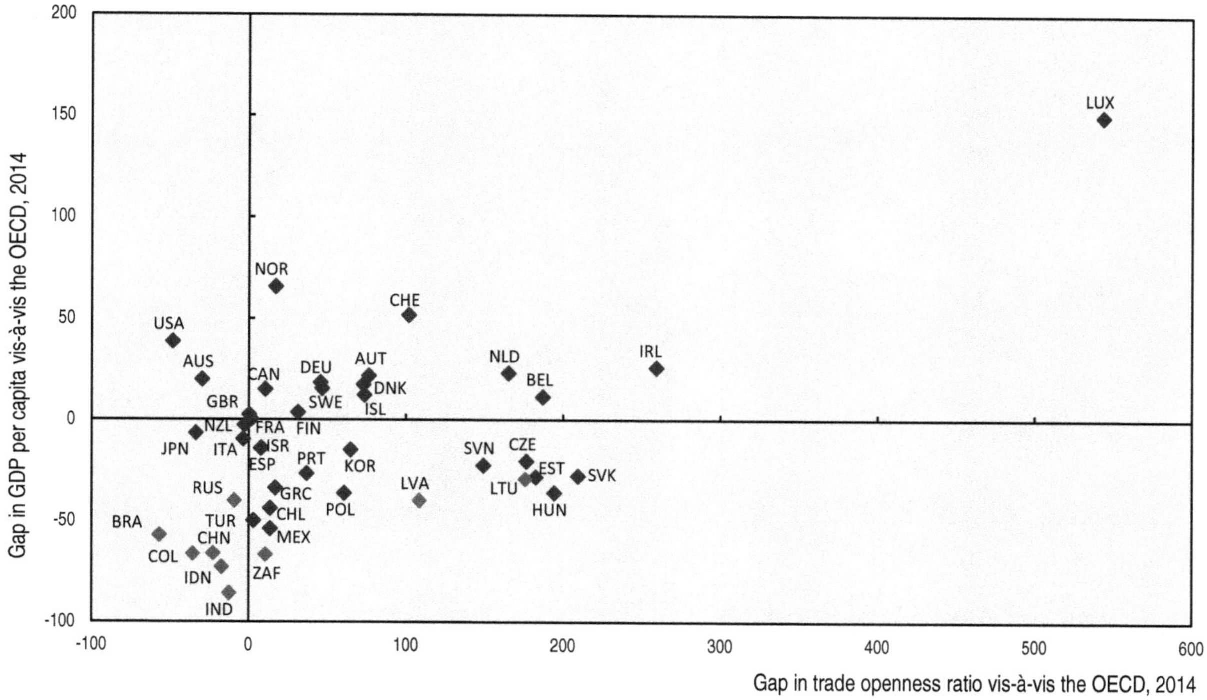

StatLink http://dx.doi.org/10.1787/888933346664

Figure 4.6. **Change in exports to GDP ratio and growth in GDP per hour worked**

Total economy, exports in gross terms (left panel) and in value added terms (right panel)

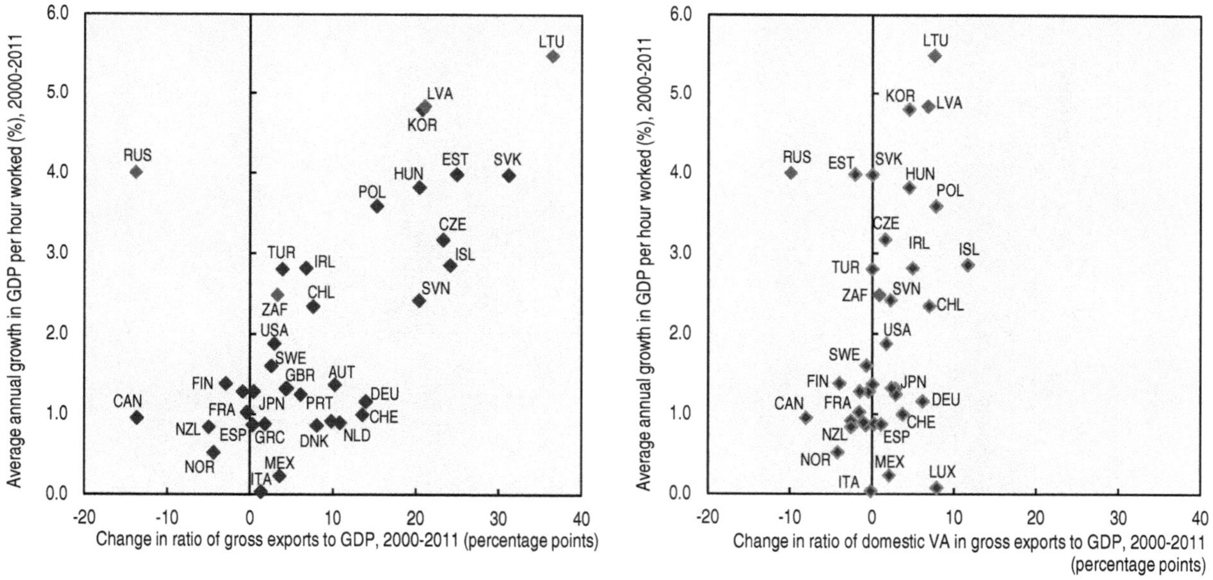

StatLink http://dx.doi.org/10.1787/888933346670

OECD Compendium of Productivity Indicators 2016

Chapter 5

Productivity trends in G7 countries

Trends in labour productivity growth

Labour productivity is a key driver of economic growth and living standards. Understanding whether the slowdown in productivity growth has been driven by structural factors and/or by reactions to the economic cycle is hence important for policy makers. This requires decomposing the time series of actual annual labour productivity growth into a trend (or structural) component and a cyclical component.

Key facts

The slowdown in labour productivity growth is a common feature of all major advanced economies and underlying long-term trends suggest that it was underway prior to the crisis. Indeed, over the 10 years preceding the crisis, trend labour productivity growth declined in all G7 countries, particularly in France, Italy and the United Kingdom. In the case of Canada, the United Kingdom and the United States, the decline since the end of the 1990s marked a reversal of growth that coincided with the IT revolution. In other countries, trend labour productivity growth has shown a gradual decline over the past 40 years from relatively high rates. The volatility in the cycle introduced by the crisis necessitates some caution in interpreting the recent trends.

Definition

Labour productivity is defined as GDP per hour worked and its growth rate is calculated as its first natural-log difference. The decomposition of labour productivity growth into a trend and a cyclical component is done by applying the Hodrick-Prescott (HP) filter (Hodrick and Prescott, 1997), where the trend component is meant to capture the long-term growth of the series and the cyclical component is the deviation from that trend. In the HP filter, the smoothness of the trend depends on a parameter usually identified as λ. The larger the value given to λ, the smoother is the trend.

Comparability

Like other filters, one limitation of the HP filter is that the estimated trend is more sensitive to transitory shocks or short-term fluctuations at the end of the sample period. This results in a sub-optimal performance of the HP filter at the endpoints of the series (Baxter and King, 1999). In view of this property, trend series are not published for the last two years for which data on actual labour productivity growth are available.

An important aspect of the HP filter is the value of the smoothing parameter λ. While for quarterly data it has been typically assumed a value of $\lambda = 1600$ (as recommended by Hodrick and Prescott, 1997), there is less agreement on the value to be used when the filter is applied to other frequencies (e.g. annual, monthly). The value of λ selected here has been determined by calibrating the Hodrick-Prescott filter in such a way that cycles shorter than 9.5 years are attenuated by 90% or more (Annex G).

Official data for Germany after unification are available only from 1991 onwards. In order to estimate data for the whole of Germany back to 1985, the Secretariat has estimated data for the whole of Germany back to 1970 by linking in 1991 the data for Germany to historical data for West Germany.

Sources and further reading

Baxter and King (1999), "Measuring business cycles: approximate band-pass filters for economic time series", *The Review of Economics and Statistics*, Vol. 81, No. 4.

Hodrick R. and E. Prescott (1997), "Postwar U.S. business cycles: An empirical investigation", *Journal of Money, Credit and Banking*, Vol. 29, No. 1.

OECD Productivity Statistics (database), *http://dx.doi.org/10.1787/pdtvy-data-en.*

OECD (2001), *Measuring Productivity – OECD Manual, http://dx.doi.org/10.1787/9789264194519-en.*

Figure 5.1. **Trend labour productivity growth in G7 countries**

Total economy, percentage change at annual rate

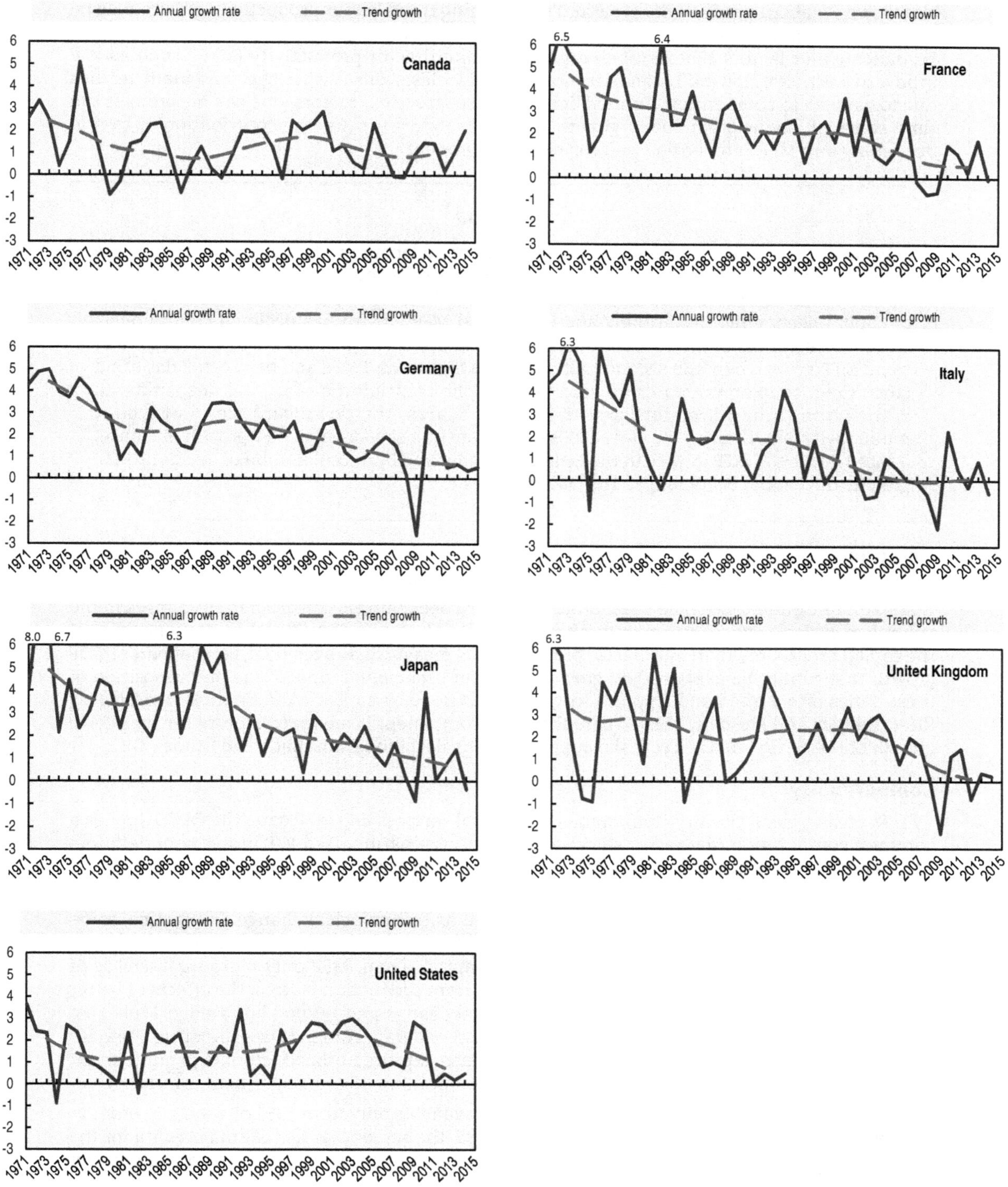

StatLink http://dx.doi.org/10.1787/888933346688

Trends in multifactor productivity and capital deepening

Policy makers are interested in the structural factors that may have accentuated the recent slowdown in labour productivity growth. The declining trend labour productivity growth may be driven by declining investment in capital relative to hours worked (capital deepening) or could be indicative of factors that hampered growth in multifactor productivity (MFP), such as low innovative activity, slow diffusion of frontier technologies, skills mismatches and inefficiencies due to barriers to competition. To shed light on these structural factors, one can decompose the time series of labour productivity growth as well as its drivers, i.e. the contribution of capital deepening and MFP, into a trend and a cyclical component.

Key facts

While nearly all G7 countries show a decline in trend labour productivity growth since the end-1990s or indeed before in some cases, the sources for this decline vary. In Canada, the downward trend of MFP growth contrasted with the flat trend observed in the contribution of capital deepening. In Germany and Italy, trend MFP growth has declined continuously since the beginning of the 1990s and flattened after the crisis. Japan saw a drastic decline in trend MFP growth over the second half of the 1980s and the 1990s and has seen a flat trend since then, coupled with a downward trend in the contribution of capital deepening. In France, the United Kingdom and the United States, the downward trend of labour productivity growth since the early 2000s was driven by a slowdown in MFP growth in France, a sharp decline in MFP growth in the United Kingdom and by a combination of declining MFP growth and capital deepening in the United States.

Definition

Labour productivity is defined as GDP per hour worked and its growth rate is calculated as its first natural-log difference. The contribution of capital deepening is constructed as changes in the volume of capital services per hour worked (i.e. capital deepening) weighted by the cost share of the capital input. Growth in multifactor productivity is measured as a residual, i.e. that part of GDP growth that cannot be explained by growth in labour and capital inputs. The decomposition of these series into a trend and a cyclical component is done by applying the Hodrick-Prescott (HP) filter (Hodrick and Prescott, 1997), where the trend component is meant to capture the long-term growth of the series and the cyclical component is the deviation from that trend (Annex G).

Comparability

To ensure cross-country comparability of capital services and MFP data, the OECD applies a common computation method to all countries that uses harmonised ICT investment deflators and assumes the same average service lives for any given asset irrespective of the country.

MFP growth is the residual part of GDP growth that cannot be explained by growth in either labour or capital input. Conceptually, it can be seen as technological change. In practice, some part of technological change, including improvements in the design and quality of new vintages of capital, is embodied in physical, notably, ICT capital. Then, MFP only picks up *disembodied* technical change, e.g., network effects or spillovers from production factors, the effects of better management practices, brand names, organisational change and general knowledge. Moreover, linked to the assumptions of the production function and data constraints hampering a precise measurement of labour and capital inputs, MFP also captures other factors, e.g. adjustment costs, economies of scale, effects from imperfect competition and measurement errors.

Official data for Germany after unification are available only from 1991 onwards. In order to estimate data for the whole of Germany back to 1985, the secretariat has estimated data for the whole of Germany back to 1970 by linking in 1991 the data for Germany to historical data for West Germany.

Sources and further reading

Hodrick R. and E. Prescott (1997), "Postwar U.S. business cycles: an empirical investigation", *Journal of Money, Credit and Banking*, Vol. 29, No. 1.

OECD Productivity Statistics (database), *http://dx.doi.org/10.1787/pdtvy-data-en.*

OECD (2001), *Measuring Productivity – OECD Manual, http://dx.doi.org/10.1787/9789264194519-en.*

Figure 5.2. **Labour productivity growth trend and its components, Canada**

Total economy, percentage change at annual rate

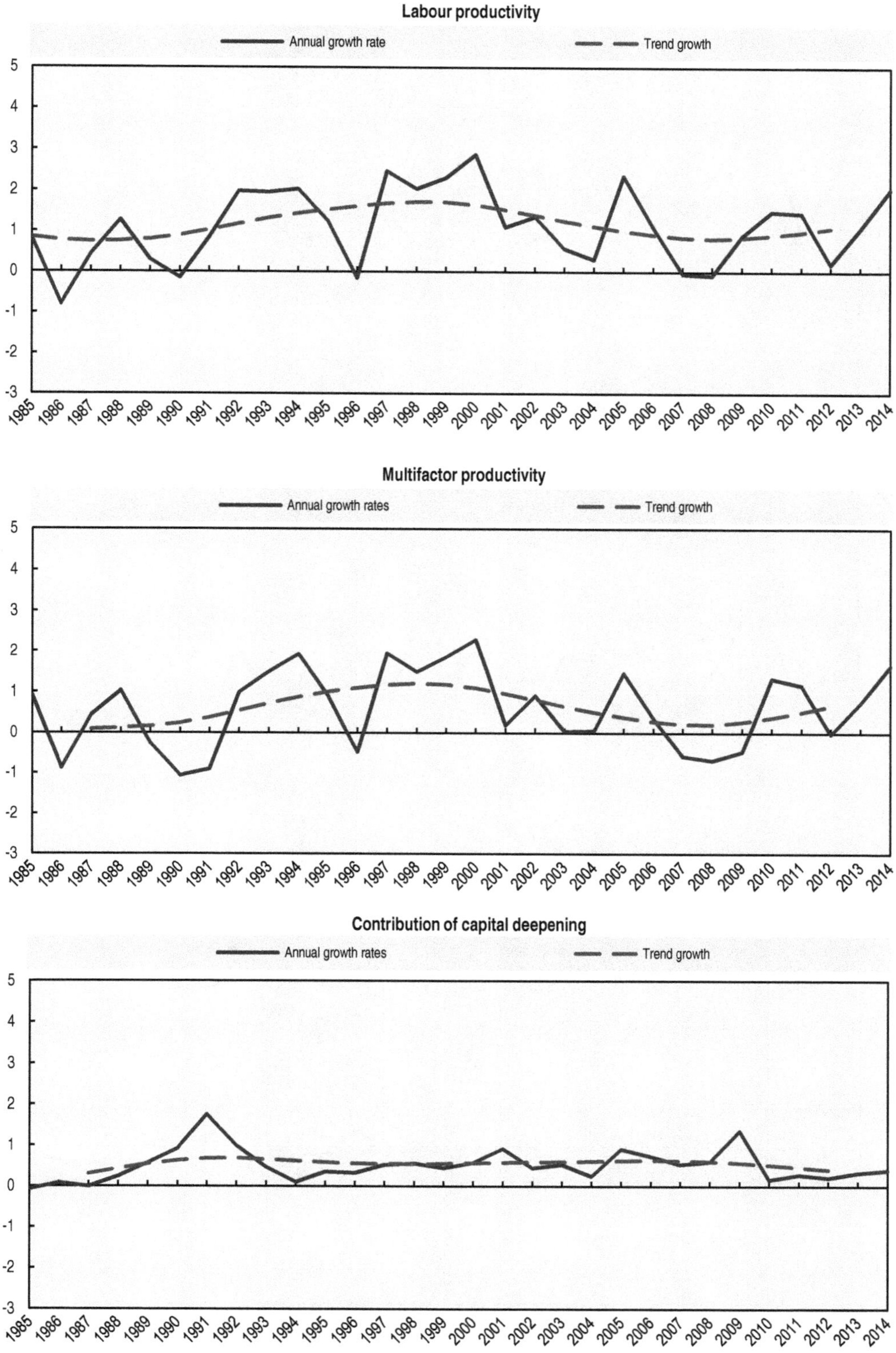

StatLink http://dx.doi.org/10.1787/888933346696

Figure 5.3. **Labour productivity growth trend and its components, France**

Total economy, percentage change at annual rate

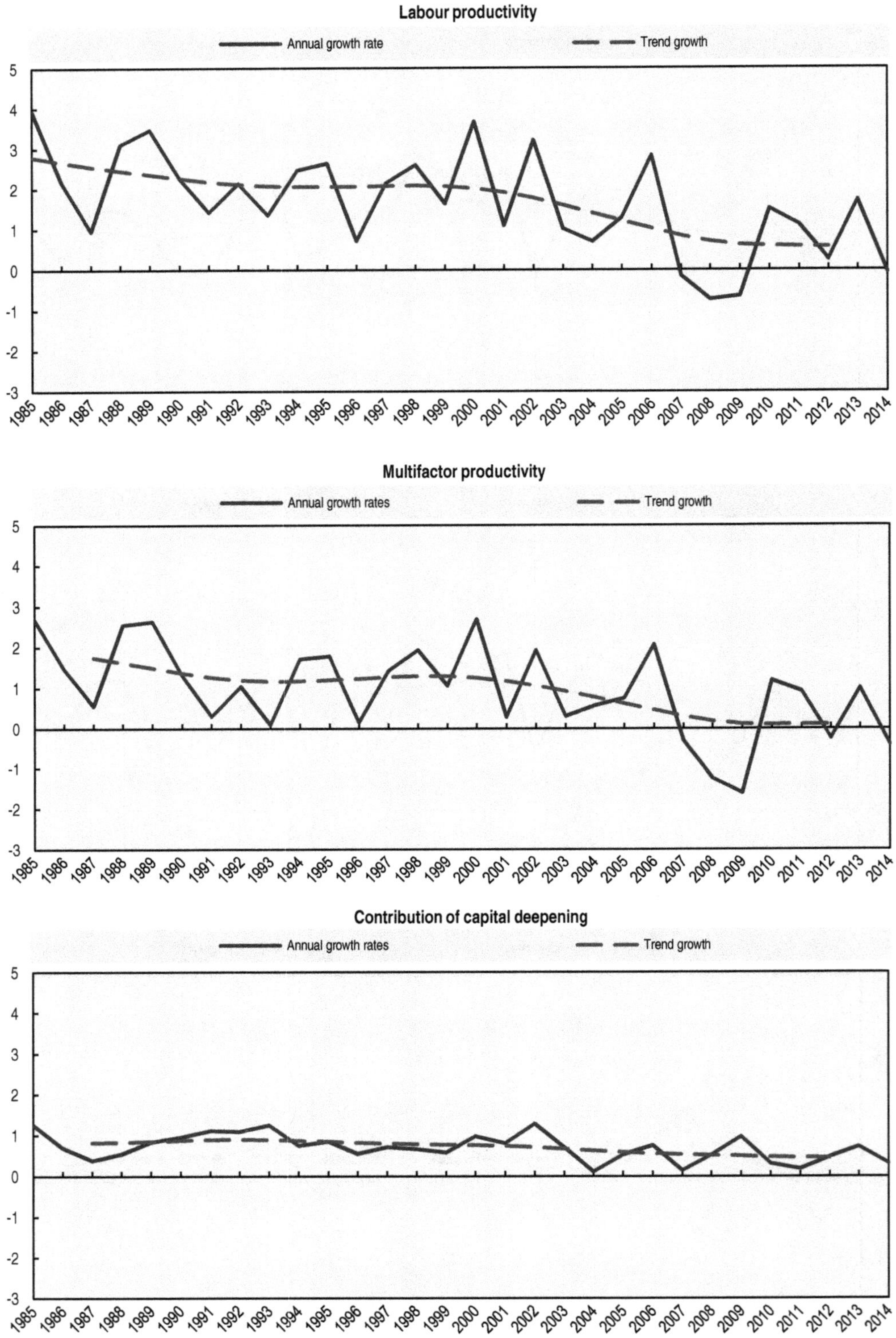

StatLink http://dx.doi.org/10.1787/888933346702

Figure 5.4. **Labour productivity growth trend and its components, Germany**

Total economy, percentage change at annual rate

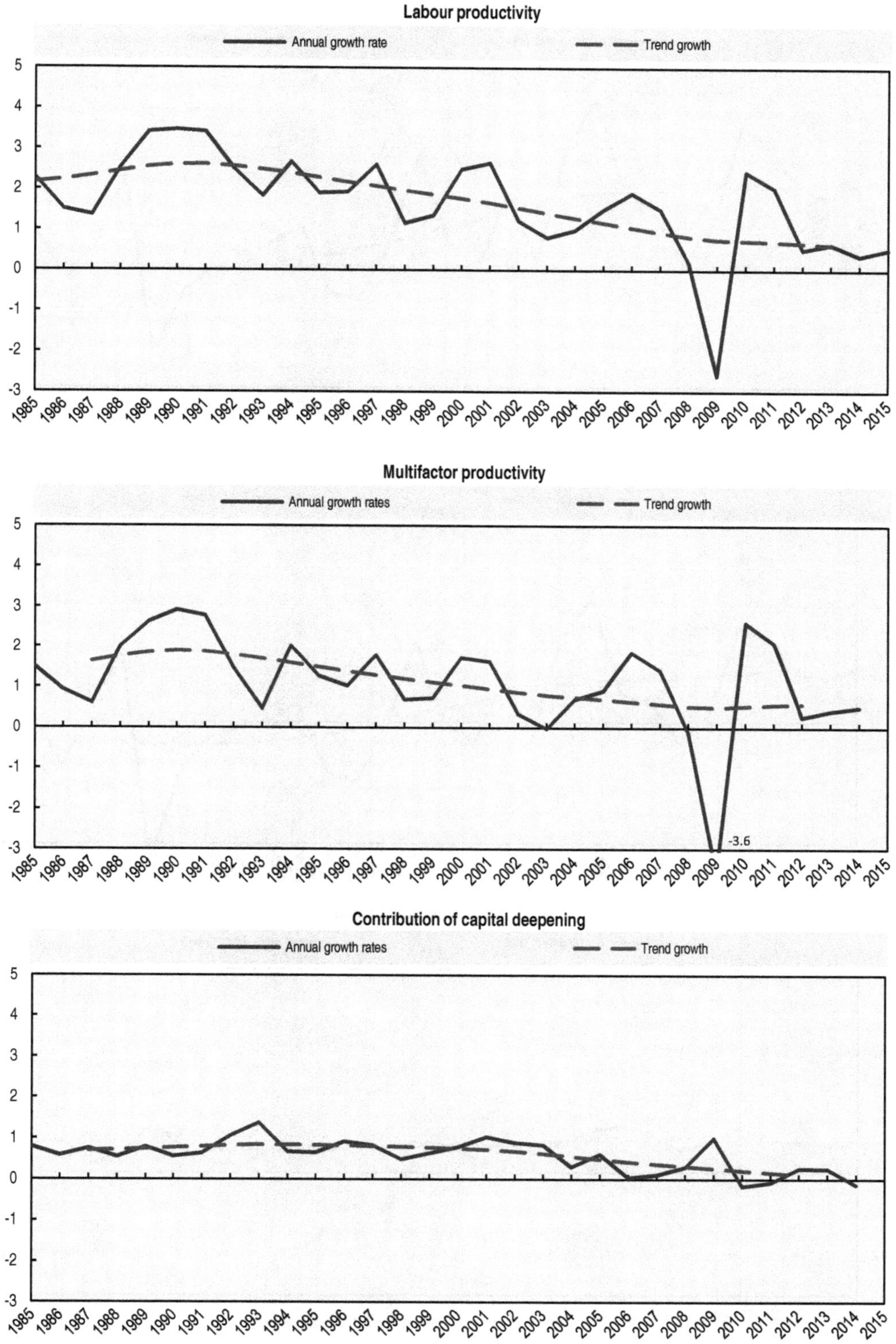

StatLink http://dx.doi.org/10.1787/888933346719

Figure 5.5. **Labour productivity growth trend and its components, Italy**

Total economy, percentage change at annual rate

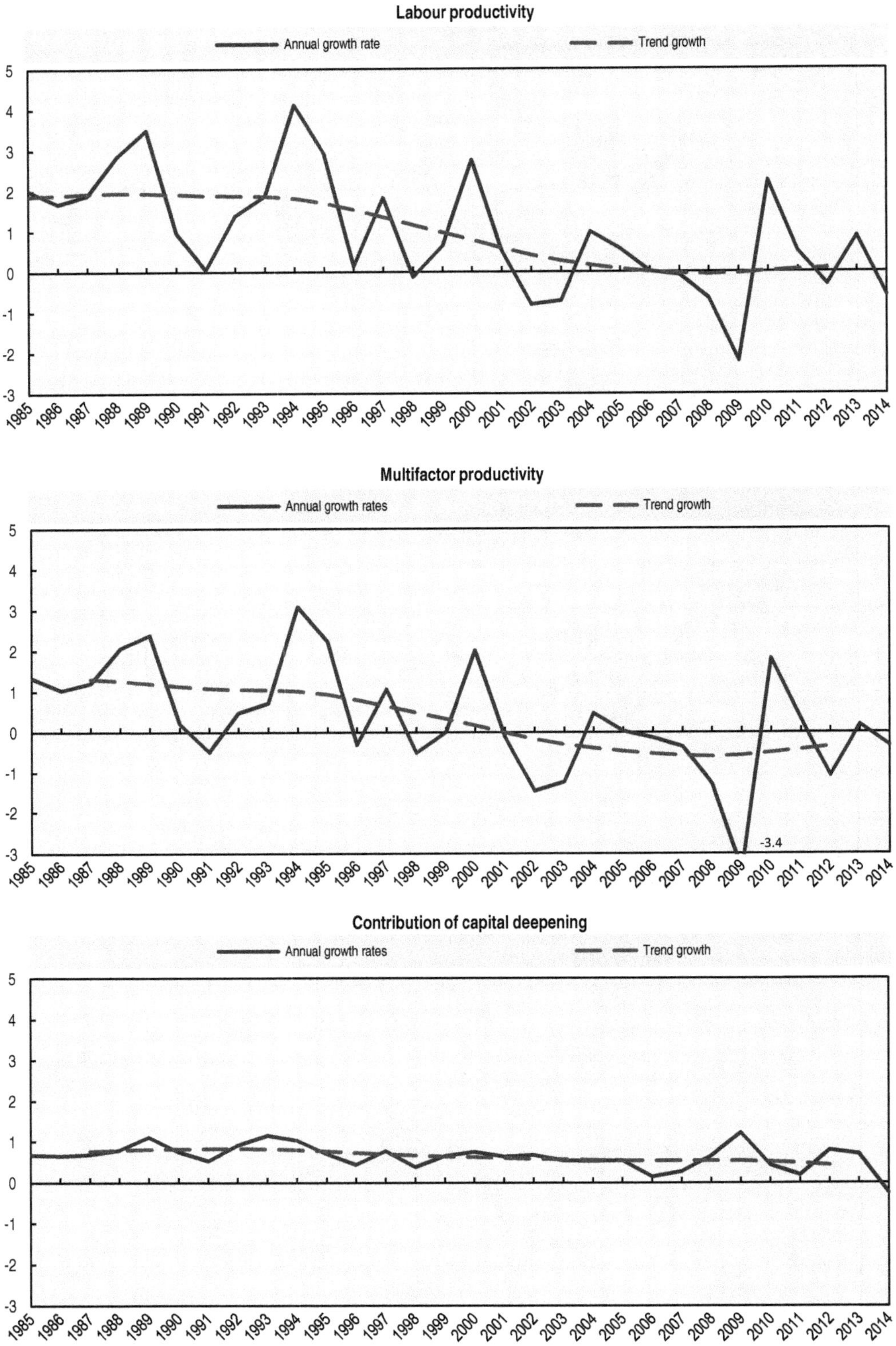

StatLink http://dx.doi.org/10.1787/888933346729

Figure 5.6. **Labour productivity growth trend and its components, Japan**

Total economy, percentage change at annual rate

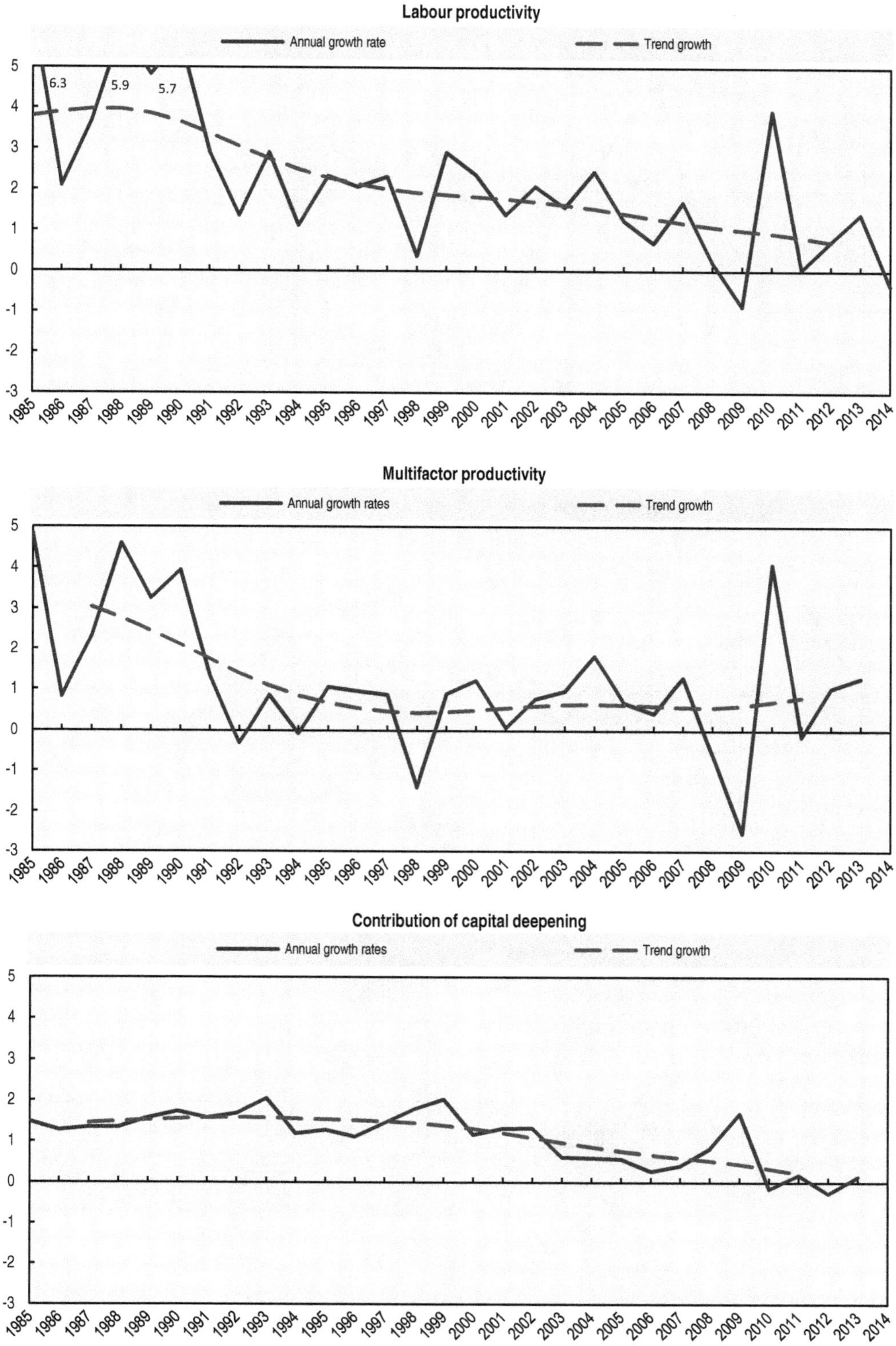

StatLink http://dx.doi.org/10.1787/888933346735

Figure 5.7. **Labour productivity growth trend and its components, United Kingdom**

Total economy, percentage change at annual rate

Labour productivity

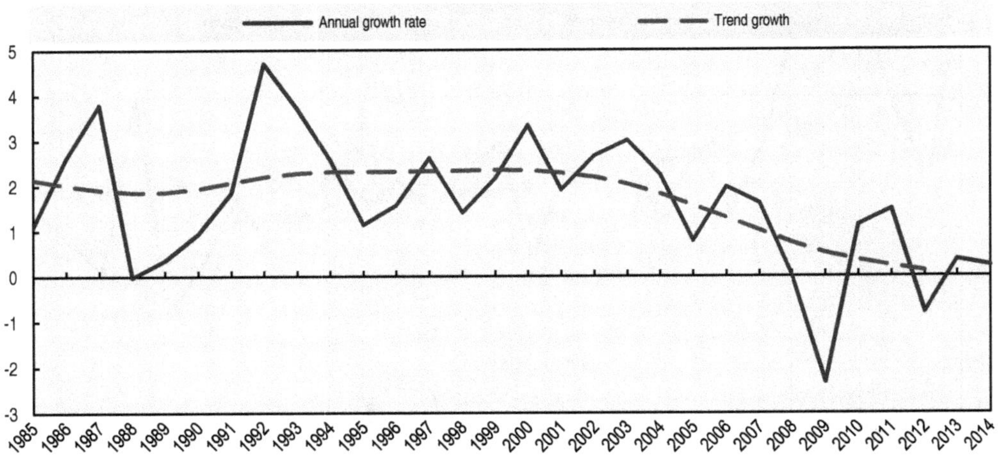

Multifactor productivity

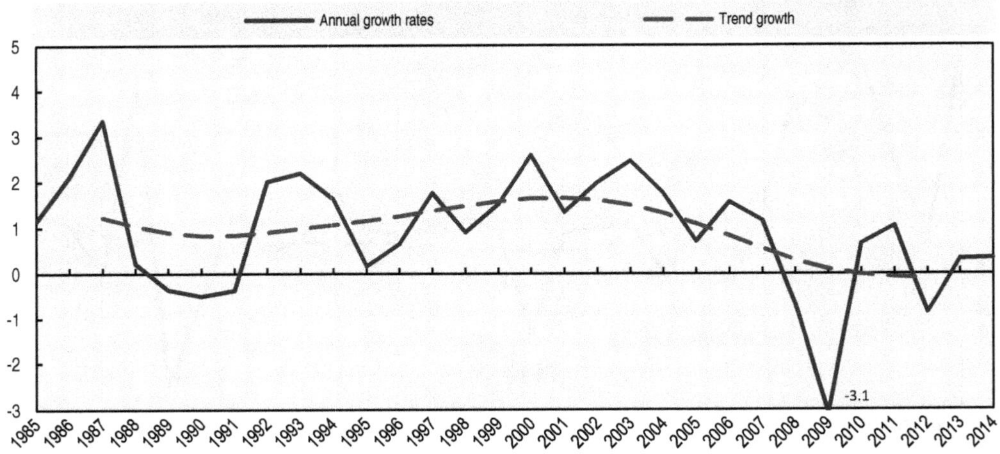

Contribution of capital deepening

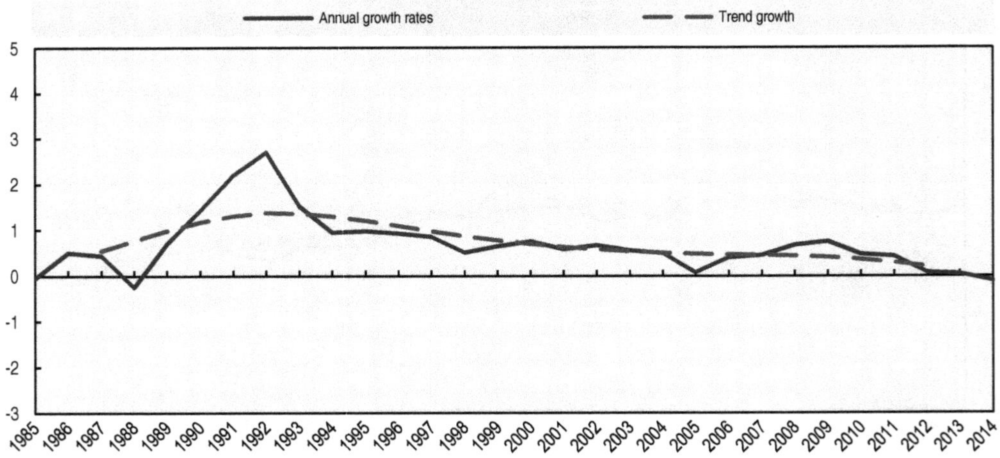

StatLink http://dx.doi.org/10.1787/888933346747

Figure 5.8. **Labour productivity growth trend and its components, United States**

Total economy, percentage change at annual rate

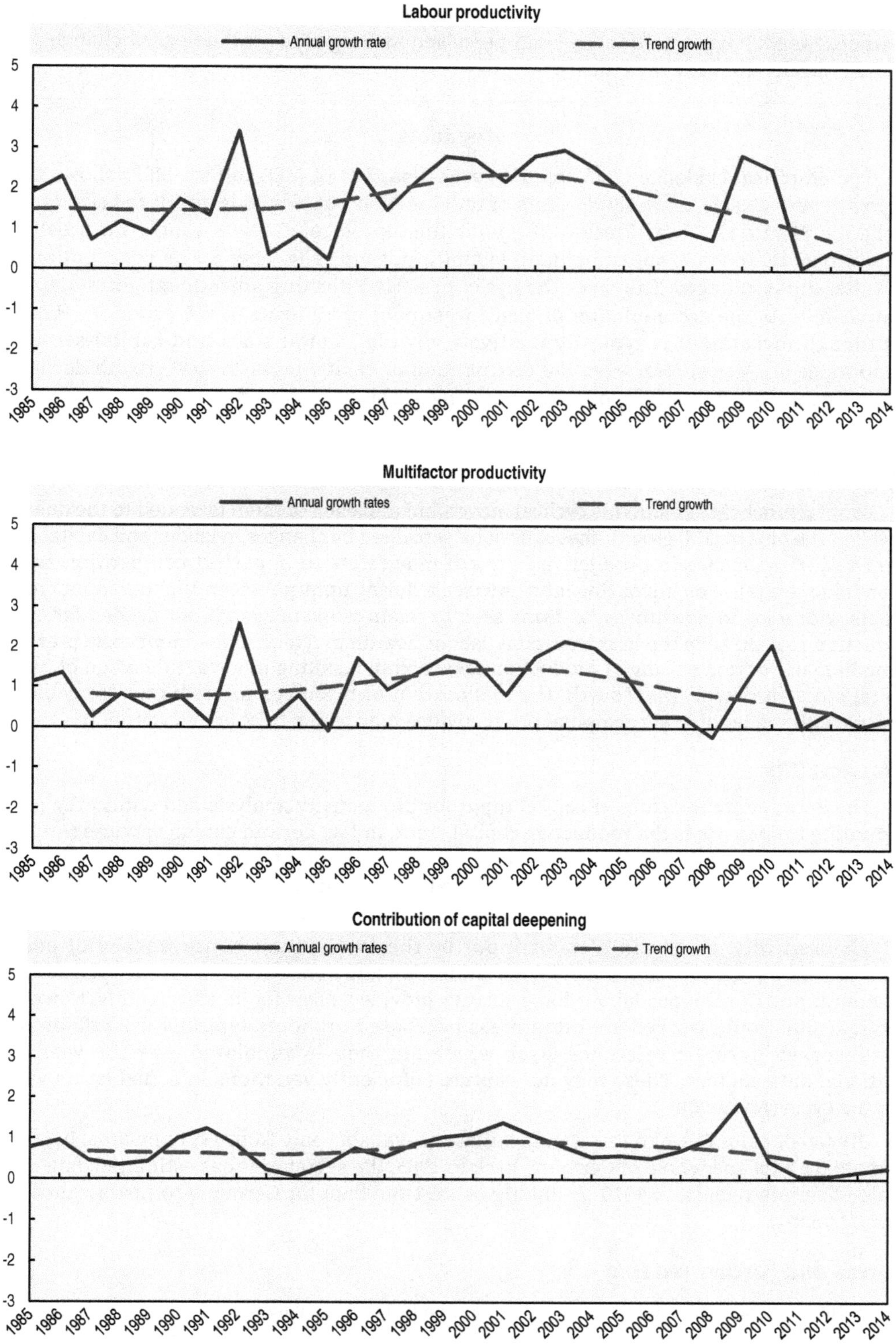

StatLink http://dx.doi.org/10.1787/888933346754

Multifactor productivity over the cycle

A number of studies indicate that multifactor productivity growth (MFP) behaves cyclically, i.e., it increases in upturns and declines in downturns. This has sometimes been interpreted as a paradox, as MFP has traditionally been perceived as exogenous technological change, which should typically not behave cyclically.

Key facts

The empirical evidence confirms the cyclical pattern of MFP. In fact, MFP follows GDP growth very closely, not only in terms of the direction but also in terms of the size of the change. While the contribution of labour fluctuated relatively strongly for most G7 countries, up to 2007, adjustments in labour input typically lagged. The contribution of capital input changed little over the cycle, possibly reflecting adjustment costs. Capital input reflects the accumulation of past investment of all firms in the economy. Hence, although investment is typically relatively volatile, capital stock and capital services estimates are less so. However, the contribution of capital input to GDP growth declined significantly after the crisis, possibly reflecting the sluggish recovery of investment.

Definitions

Four factors help explain this cyclical movement and each of them is related to the definition of MFP as the part of GDP growth that cannot be explained by changes in labour and capital inputs (Annex A). First, cycles in productivity growth may relate to imperfect competition and the potential to capitalise on increasing returns to scale during upturns. Second, labour input typically adjusts with a lag in downturns, as firms seek to retain workers even if not needed for current production so as to keep the human capital (labour hoarding). Third, adjustment costs prevent an immediate up- or downsizing of production and capital, resulting in lower utilisation of existing capital stock in downturns. Fourth, the reallocation of resources to production of goods and services with higher or lower marginal productivities may be pro or counter cyclical.

Comparability

The appropriate measure of capital input for productivity analysis and within the growth accounting framework is the productive capital stock and its derived capital services (Annex C). While these take into account the productivity of the different capital assets, no account is taken of the extent to which the existing capital stock is actually used, i.e. the rate of capital utilisation, which may affect comparability over time and space.

Theoretically, measuring labour input by the total actual hours worked of persons employed should capture the rate of labour utilisation and hence account for the cyclical effects of labour input. Continuous labour force surveys provide a basis for measuring this. However in practice, total hours worked are often measured based on hours typically worked, or actual hours worked during a reference week which are then extrapolated over the year using additional data sources. These may not capture sufficiently variations in actual hours worked over the cycle (Annex B).

Official data for Germany after unification are available only from 1991 onwards. In order to estimate data for the whole of Germany back to 1985, the secretariat has estimated data for the whole of Germany back to 1970 by linking in 1991 the data for Germany to historical data for West Germany.

Sources and further reading

OECD Productivity Statistics (database), *http://dx.doi.org/10.1787/pdtvy-data-en.*

OECD (2001), *Measuring Productivity – OECD Manual, http://dx.doi.org/10.1787/9789264194519-en.*

OECD (2009), *Measuring Capital – OECD Manual, http://dx.doi.org/10.1787/9789264068476-en.*

Wölfl, A. and D. Hajkova (2007), "Measuring Multifactor Productivity Growth", *OECD STI Working Papers* 2007/05, *http://dx.doi.org/10.1787/246367010342.*

Figure 5.9. **Contributions to GDP growth over time in G7 countries**

Total economy, percentage point contributions at annual rate

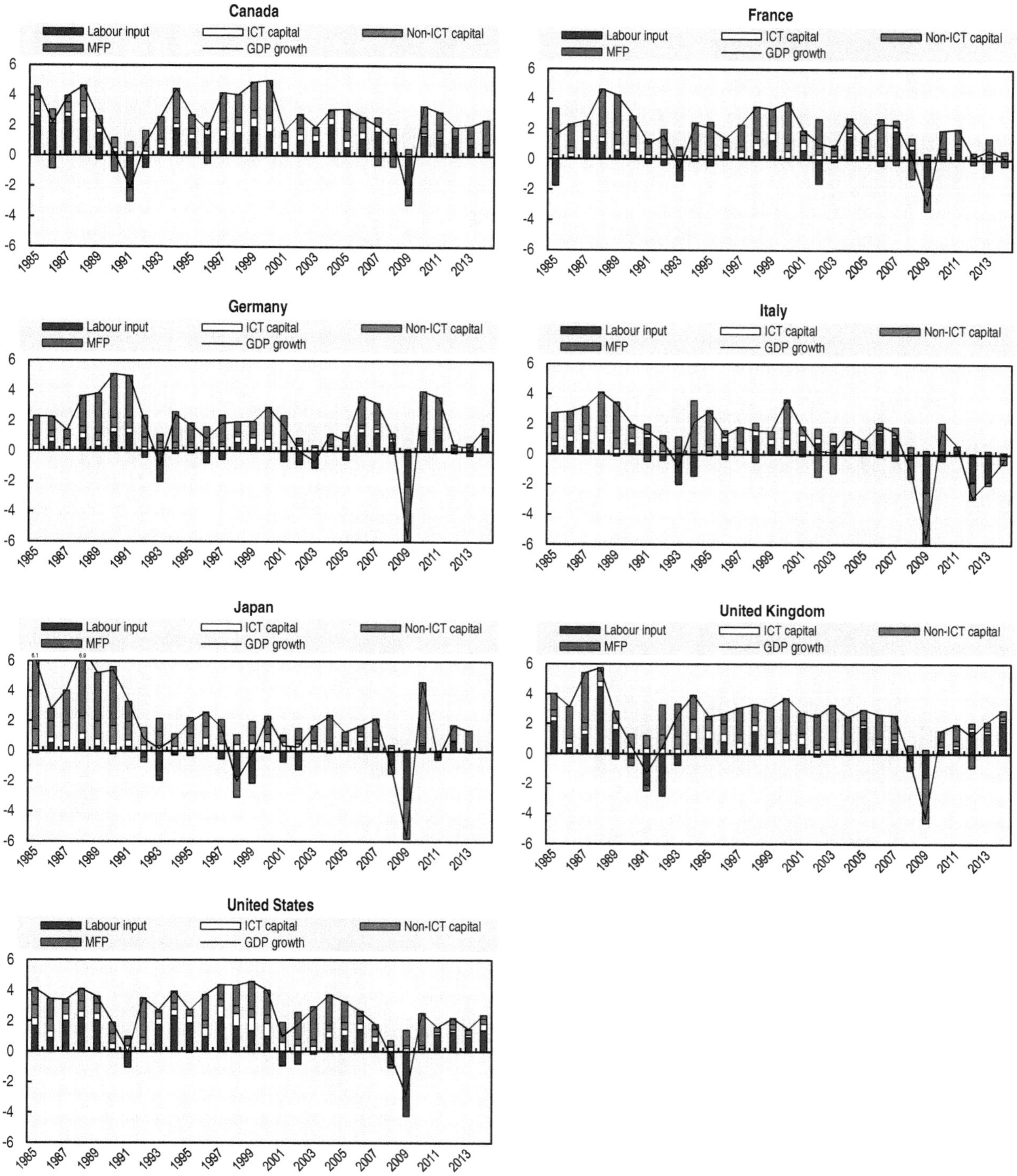

StatLink http://dx.doi.org/10.1787/888933346760

Methodological annexes

ANNEX A

Productivity measures

The *OECD Productivity Statistics* (database) (PDB) contains a consistent set of productivity measures at the total economy and at the industry levels. This annex provides detailed information on the measures included in the database. While the PDB and this publication present value added based productivity indicators by relating value added to the labour and capital inputs used, productivity measures can be computed for different representations of the production process. One typical approach is to relate a volume measure of gross output to primary and intermediate inputs, as used in the KLEMS methodology, which measures the contributions of capital (K), labour (L), energy (E), material inputs (M) and services (S) to output growth. This representation is not adopted in the PDB nor in this publication.

Productivity measures for the total economy

Labour input

Within the PDB, labour input (L) is defined as total hours worked of all persons engaged in production (i.e. employees plus self-employed). The preferred source for total hours worked is the OECD *National Accounts Statistics* (database). However, this database does not provide data on hours worked for all countries, and, so, other sources are necessarily used, e.g. the *OECD Employment and Labour Market Statistics* (database). Estimates of average hours actually worked per year per person employed are also provided within the PDB. Annex B presents detailed information on hours worked.

Capital input

Capital input (K) is measured as the volume of capital services, which is the appropriate measure for capital input within the growth accounting framework (see Schreyer et al., 2003 for more details on the computation of capital services). In the PDB, capital services measures are based on productive capital stocks derived using the perpetual inventory method (PIM). The PIM calculations are carried out by the OECD, using an assumption of common service lives for given assets for all countries, and by correcting for differences in the national deflators used for information and communication technology (ICT) assets. The investment series by type of asset are sourced from national statistical offices.

From 2015, the classification of assets adopted in the PDB is in line with the SNA 2008. Capital services are computed separately for eight non-residential fixed assets $k = 1, 2, \ldots, 8$, i.e. computer hardware, telecommunications equipment, transport equipment, other machinery and equipment and weapons systems, non-residential construction, computer software and databases, research and development and other intellectual property products. The volume index of total capital services is computed by aggregating the volume change of capital services of all individual assets using a Törnqvist index that applies asset specific user cost shares as weights:

$$\ln\left(\frac{K^t}{K^{t-1}}\right)=\sum_{k=1}^{8}\frac{1}{2}\left(v_k^t+v_k^{t-1}\right)\ln\left(\frac{K_k^t}{K_k^{t-1}}\right)$$

where:

$$v_k^t=\left(\frac{u_k^t K_k^t}{\sum_{k=1}^{8}u_k^t K_k^t}\right)$$

and u_k^t is the user cost per unit of capital services provided by asset k at time t (see Schreyer et al., 2003). Thereby, v_k^t is the user cost share of asset k, $\frac{1}{2}\left(v_k^t+v_k^{t-1}\right)\ln\left(\frac{K_k^t}{K_k^{t-1}}\right)$ is the contribution of asset k to total capital services in year t and K_k^t is the quantity of capital services provided by asset k in year t.

Aggregate volume indices of capital services are also computed for ICT assets (computer hardware, telecommunications equipment and computer software and databases) and non-ICT assets (transport equipment, other machinery and equipment and weapons systems, non-residential construction, research and development and other intellectual property products), using the appropriate user costs shares as weights. The aggregate volume indices of ICT and non-ICT capital services are given by:

$$\ln\left(\frac{K_{ict}^t}{K_{ict}^{t-1}}\right)=\sum_{i=1}^{3}\frac{1}{2}\left(\gamma_i^t+\gamma_i^{t-1}\right)\ln\left(\frac{K_i^t}{K_i^{t-1}}\right)$$

where i represents an ICT asset and

$$\gamma_i^t=\left(\frac{u_i^t K_i^t}{\sum_{i=1}^{3}u_i^t K_i^t}\right)$$

$$\ln\left(\frac{K_{nict}^t}{K_{nict}^{t-1}}\right)=\sum_{j=1}^{5}\frac{1}{2}\left(\gamma_j^t+\gamma_j^{t-1}\right)\ln\left(\frac{K_j^t}{K_j^{t-1}}\right)$$

where j represents a non-ICT asset and

$$\gamma_j^t=\left(\frac{u_j^t K_j^t}{\sum_{j=1}^{5}u_j^t K_j^t}\right)$$

Cost shares of inputs

The total cost of inputs is the sum of the labour input cost and the total cost of capital services. The national accounts record the income of the self-employed *as mixed income*. This includes the compensation of both labour and capital. As such, in the PDB total labour input costs for the self-employed and employees are computed as the average remuneration per employee multiplied by the total number of persons employed. The preferred source for data on compensation of employees and for the number of employees as well as the number of self-employed is the *OECD National Accounts Statistics* (database). Whenever these data are not available in the *OECD National Accounts Statistics* (database), other sources are used, i.e. the *OECD Employment and Labour Market Statistics* (database) and national statistical authorities.

The labour input cost is calculated as follows:

$$w^t L^t = \left(\frac{COMP^t}{EE^t}\right) E^t$$

where $w^t L^t$ reflects the total remuneration for labour input in period t, $COMP^t$ is the total compensation of employees in period t, EE^t is the number of employees in period t, and E^t the total number of employed persons, i.e., employees plus self-employed, in period t.

Total capital input cost is computed as the sum of the user costs of each capital asset type k given by $u_k^t K_k^t$, where u_k^t is the user cost per unit of capital services provided by asset type k.

The total cost of inputs is then given by

$$C^t = w^t L^t + \sum_{k=1}^{8} u_k^t K_k^t$$

and the corresponding cost shares of labour and capital are

$s_L^t \equiv \frac{w^t L^t}{C^t}$ for labour input,

$s_K^t \equiv \frac{\sum_{k=1}^{8} u_k^t K_k^t}{C^t}$ for total capital input,

$s_{K_{ict}}^t \equiv \frac{\sum_{i=1}^{3} u_i^t K_i^t}{C^t}$ for capital input derived from ICT assets i=1,2,3,

$s_{K_{nict}}^t \equiv \frac{\sum_{j=1}^{5} u_j^t K_j^t}{C^t}$ for capital input derived from non-ICT assets j=1,…, 5.

Labour productivity

At the total economy level, labour productivity is measured as Gross domestic product (GDP) at market prices and at constant prices per hour worked.

Multifactor productivity

In simple terms, growth in multifactor productivity (MFP) can be described as the change in output that cannot be explained by changes in the quantity of capital and labour inputs used to generate output. In the PDB it is measured by deducting the growth of labour and capital inputs from output growth as follows:

$$\ln\left(\frac{MFP^t}{MFP^{t-1}}\right) = \ln\left(\frac{Q^t}{Q^{t-1}}\right) - \ln\left(\frac{X^t}{X^{t-1}}\right)$$

where Q is output measured as GDP at market prices and at constant prices. X relates to total inputs used and the rate of change of these inputs is calculated as a weighted average of the rate of change of labour and capital inputs, with the respective cost shares as weights. Aggregation of these inputs is by way of the Törnqvist index:

$$\ln\left(\frac{X^t}{X^{t-1}}\right) = \frac{1}{2}\left(s_L^t + s_L^{t-1}\right)\ln\left(\frac{L^t}{L^{t-1}}\right) + \frac{1}{2}\left(s_K^t + s_K^{t-1}\right)\ln\left(\frac{K^t}{K^{t-1}}\right)$$

Contributions to GDP growth

In the growth accounting framework, GDP growth can be decomposed into the contributions of each production factor plus multifactor productivity:

$$\ln\left(\frac{Q^t}{Q^{t-1}}\right)=\frac{1}{2}\left(s_L^t+s_L^{t-1}\right)\ln\left(\frac{L^t}{L^{t-1}}\right)+\frac{1}{2}\left(s_{K_{ict}}^t+s_{K_{ict}}^{t-1}\right)\ln\left(\frac{K_{ict}^t}{K_{ict}^{t-1}}\right)+\frac{1}{2}\left(s_{K_{nict}}^t+s_{K_{nict}}^{t-1}\right)\ln\left(\frac{K_{nict}^t}{K_{nict}^{t-1}}\right)+\ln\left(\frac{MFP^t}{MFP^{t-1}}\right)$$

where:

$\frac{1}{2}\left(s_L^t+s_L^{t-1}\right)\ln\left(\frac{L^t}{L^{t-1}}\right)$ is the contribution of labour input to GDP growth,

$\frac{1}{2}\left(s_{K_{ict}}^t+s_{K_{ict}}^{t-1}\right)\ln\left(\frac{K_{ict}^t}{K_{ict}^{t-1}}\right)$ is the contribution of ICT capital input to GDP growth,

$\frac{1}{2}\left(s_{K_{nict}}^t+s_{K_{nict}}^{t-1}\right)\ln\left(\frac{K_{nict}^t}{K_{nict}^{t-1}}\right)$ is the contribution of non-ICT capital input to GDP growth.

Contributions to labour productivity growth

By reformulating the decomposition of output growth presented above, it is possible to decompose labour productivity growth into the contribution of capital deepening and MFP.

$$\ln\left(\frac{LP^t}{LP^{t-1}}\right)=\frac{1}{2}\left(s_K^t+s_K^{t-1}\right)\left[\ln\left(\frac{K^t}{K^{t-1}}\right)-\ln\left(\frac{L^t}{L^{t-1}}\right)\right]+\ln\left(\frac{MFP^t}{MFP^{t-1}}\right)$$

where:

$\ln\left(\frac{LP^t}{LP^{t-1}}\right)=\ln\left(\frac{Q^t}{Q^{t-1}}\right)-\ln\left(\frac{L^t}{L^{t-1}}\right)$ is labour productivity growth,

$\ln\left(\frac{K^t}{K^{t-1}}\right)-\ln\left(\frac{L^t}{L^{t-1}}\right)$ is capital deepening (i.e. growth in capital services per hour worked),

$\frac{1}{2}\left(s_K^t+s_K^{t-1}\right)\left[\ln\left(\frac{K^t}{K^{t-1}}\right)-\ln\left(\frac{L^t}{L^{t-1}}\right)\right]$ is the contribution of capital deepening to labour productivity growth.

It is also possible to reformulate the decomposition of labour productivity growth to show the contributions of ICT capital and non-ICT capital:

$$\ln\left(\frac{LP^t}{LP^{t-1}}\right)=\frac{1}{2}\left(s_{K_{ict}}^t+s_{K_{ict}}^{t-1}\right)\left[\ln\left(\frac{K_{ict}^t}{K_{ict}^{t-1}}\right)-\ln\left(\frac{L^t}{L^{t-1}}\right)\right]+\frac{1}{2}\left(s_{K_{nict}}^t+s_{K_{nict}}^{t-1}\right)\left[\ln\left(\frac{K_{nict}^t}{K_{nict}^{t-1}}\right)-\ln\left(\frac{L^t}{L^{t-1}}\right)\right]+\ln\left(\frac{MFP^t}{MFP^{t-1}}\right)$$

where:

$\frac{1}{2}\left(s_{K_{ict}}^t+s_{K_{ict}}^{t-1}\right)\left[\ln\left(\frac{K_{ict}^t}{K_{ict}^{t-1}}\right)-\ln\left(\frac{L^t}{L^{t-1}}\right)\right]$ is the contribution of ICT capital to labour productivity growth,

$\frac{1}{2}\left(s_{K_{nict}}^t+s_{K_{nict}}^{t-1}\right)\left[\ln\left(\frac{K_{nict}^t}{K_{nict}^{t-1}}\right)-\ln\left(\frac{L^t}{L^{t-1}}\right)\right]$ is the contribution of non-ICT capital to labour productivity growth.

Unit labour costs and their components

Unit labour costs (ULC) measure the average cost of labour per unit of output produced. They are calculated as the ratio of total labour costs to real output. At the total economy level, real output is measured as GDP at market prices and constant prices. Equivalently, ULCs may be expressed as the ratio of total labour costs per hour worked to GDP per hour worked, i.e., labour productivity.

In principle, the appropriate numerator for ULC calculations is total labour costs of all persons engaged. In practice, however, this information is not readily available for most countries. As such, OECD total labour cost estimates used in calculating ULCs are based on adjusted estimates of compensation of employees (COE), compiled according to the System of National Accounts (SNA).

Compensation of employees as defined in the SNA excludes labour compensation for the self-employed which is covered in the item *mixed income*. However, the output of the self-employed contributes to value added, and, so, the OECD estimates of total labour costs include explicit adjustments to capture the labour compensation component of mixed income. This adjustment is made by multiplying compensation of employees by the ratio of hours worked for total employment to hours worked of employees.

The adjustment for the self-employed assumes that labour compensation per hour or per person is equivalent for the self-employed and employees of businesses. This assumption may be more or less valid across different countries.

Productivity measures at industry level

The conceptual approach used to estimate productivity at industry level follows that for the total economy. However the same quantity (and quality) of data that is available for the whole economy estimates is not always available at the detailed industry level. Hence some approximations are necessary and, so, some differences may prevail between the whole economy estimates and those at industry level.

Productivity measures at industry level are computed for 14 industries (activities), each defined in accordance with the International Standard Industry Classification (ISIC) Rev. 4.

Labour input

Labour input is measured as total hours worked by all persons engaged in production, i.e. employees plus self-employed, broken down by industry.

Labour productivity

At the industry level, labour productivity is measured as gross value added at basic prices and constant prices per hour worked.

Contributions to labour productivity growth

The contribution of an economic activity to labour productivity growth of a group of economic activities (e.g. total business sector, total services) is compiled as follows using a Törnqvist index:

$$Cont(i,t) = \frac{1}{2}\left[\left(\frac{Q_{cur,i,t}}{Q_{cur,tot,t}} + \frac{Q_{cur,i,t-1}}{Q_{cur,tot,t-1}}\right)\theta_t\left(Q_{con,i}\right) - \left(\frac{L_{i,t}}{L_{tot,t}} + \frac{L_{i,t-1}}{L_{tot,t-1}}\right)\theta_t\left(L_i\right)\right]$$

where:

i is an economic activity,

tot is an aggregate of economic activities including economic activity i,

Q_{cur} is gross value added at current prices,

Q_{con} is gross value added at constant prices,

L is the number of hours worked,

$\theta_t(x)$ is the annual growth rate of x between time t-1 and t.

Unit labour costs and their components

Unit labour costs (ULC) measure the average cost of labour per unit of output produced. They are calculated as the ratio of total labour costs to real output. For main economic activities, real output is measured as gross value added at basic prices and constant prices. Equivalently, ULCs may be expressed as the ratio of total labour costs per hour worked to gross value added per hour worked, i.e., labour productivity.

Total labour costs used for the calculations of ULCs by economic activity are computed as described above for the total economy.

References

OECD (2001), *Measuring Productivity – OECD Manual: Measurement of Aggregate and Industry-Level Productivity Growth*, OECD Publishing, Paris, *http://dx.doi.org/10.1787/9789264194519-en.*

OECD (2009), *Measuring Capital – OECD Manual, Second edition,* OECD Publishing, Paris, *http://dx.doi.org/10.1787/9789264068476-en.*

Schreyer, P. (2004), "Capital Stocks, Capital Services and Multi-Factor Productivity Measures", *OECD Economic Studies*, Vol. 2003/2, *http://dx.doi.org/10.1787/eco_studies-v2003-art11-en.*

Schreyer, P., P. Bignon and J. Dupont (2003), "OECD Capital Services Estimates: Methodology and a First Set of Results", *OECD Statistics Working Papers*, No. 2003/06, OECD Publishing, Paris, *http://dx.doi.org/10.1787/658687860232.*

ANNEX B

Measuring hours worked

Hours worked for productivity analysis – main definitions

Within the *OECD Productivity Statistics* (database) (PDB), the underlying concept for labour input is *total hours actually worked by all persons engaged in production*. It is instructive to consider the relationship between this concept and related measures of working time (Table B.1):

- *Hours actually worked* – hours actually spent on productive activities;
- *Hours usually worked* – the typical hours worked during a short reference period such as a week over a longer observation period;
- *Hours paid for* – the hours worked for which remuneration is paid;
- *Contractual hours of work* – the hours time that individuals are expected to work based on work contracts;
- *Overtime hours of work* – the hours actually worked in excess of contractual hours; and
- *Absence from work hours* – the hours that persons are expected to work but do not work.

Table B.1. **Relationship between different concepts of hours worked**

Overtime hours of work					Absences from work			
Irregular overtime		Regular overtime			Irregular absence		Regular absence	
Unpaid	*Paid*	*Paid*	*Unpaid*		*Unpaid*	*Paid*	*Paid*	*Unpaid*
				Contractual hours				
				Hours actually worked				
				Hours usually worked				
				Hours paid for				

Note: Establishing the relationship between normal hours and the five other concepts is not possible, as normal hours are established on a case-by-case basis.
Source: ILO (2008), Measurement of working time, 18th ICLS.

Because productivity analysis is interested in measuring the inputs used in producing a given output, the underlying concept for labour input should include all hours used in production, whether paid or not. They should exclude those hours not used in production, even if some compensation is received for those hours. As such the relevant concept for measuring labour input is *hours actually worked*. The productive or non-productive characteristic of an activity is determined by its inclusion in, or exclusion from, the SNA production boundary. *Hours actually worked* are defined as (ILO, 2008):

- the hours spent directly on productive activities or in activities in relation to them (maintenance time, cleaning time, training time, waiting time, time spent on call duty, travelling time between work locations);
- the time spent in between these hours when the person continues to be available for work (for reasons that are either inherent to the job or due to temporary interruptions); and
- short resting time.

Conversely, *hours actually worked* should exclude:

- annual leave and public holidays;
- longer breaks from work (*e.g.* meal breaks);
- commuting time (when no productive activity is performed); and
- educational activities other than on-the-job training time.

Measuring hours worked

In general, *Labour Force Surveys* (LFS) are the main source used to compile hours worked data in a majority of countries. LFS is most often also the principal underlying source in *National Accounts* – the main source ultimately used in the *OECD Productivity Statistics* (database) LFS include questions on the number of hours actually and usually worked in the reference period, and questions concerning the differences between the time usually spent working and the time actually worked during the reference week. Additional LFS questions concerning working time components such as work at home, commuting time, short breaks, overtime and absence from work are also often available.

Continuous labour force surveys are especially appropriate for measuring working time as they allow direct collection of data on hours actually worked throughout the year. This method is known as the *direct method*, as it is based on a direct measure of average actual hours of work during each week of the year, effectively taking into account all types of absences from work and overtime.

However, in most cases, LFS are not continuous and so that the *direct method* to measure actual hours worked during the year is not applicable. In these cases, estimates are built using the *component method*. Thereby, data are collected for a specific reference week (e.g. one week during a month) and complemented with other data to build annual estimates of actual hours worked during the year. The component method starts with the usual hours of work collected in the LFS and then adjusts for absences from work such as holidays, bank holidays, illness, maternity leave, overtime, etc. Annual totals are then derived by scaling up the weekly estimate.

In some countries, LFS are not used or are complemented with information from other sources. Among such other sources are the following:

1. *Establishment (and enterprise) surveys*. These are typically the main source of information for hours worked estimates by industry. One of the main drawbacks of this source is that the data collected generally refer to hours *paid* rather than actual hours *worked*, hence include paid absences and exclude unpaid overtime.

2. *Administrative records,* such as social security and tax registers. These are the main sources of information for adjusting data from labour force surveys and establishment surveys to obtain estimates of absences from work due to illness, maternity leave, occupational injuries, strikes and lockouts.
3. *Time Use Surveys.* These are useful to compare the results from other sources but their irregularity, low frequency and limited international comparability is a drawback. Labour force survey based estimates of working time typically over-report hours worked when compared with estimates from time use surveys.

For productivity analysis, consistency of LFS based data on hours worked with the *National Accounts* concepts needs to be ensured (OECD, 2009; Ypma and van Ark, 2006). This implies adjusting the coverage of activities included in the LFS to that used to compute GDP, and adapting the geographical and economic boundaries of employment to GDP. The notion of economic territory used to compute GDP refers to the domestic concept, i.e. resident persons working outside the country are excluded. Some of these adjustments can be considered as negligible for most countries although they are made in all countries. Likewise, measures of hours actually worked should refer to productive activities within the SNA production boundaries (by definition); persons spending time on productive activities excluded from the original sources should therefore be included.

In general, when LFS is the main source of information for employment, adjustments concern persons outside the LFS universe but who need to be included as persons engaged in production, as defined in the SNA. The causes for differences between these two measures are:

- age threshold (e.g. people under 15 engaged in production are generally not included in LFS estimates);
- non-coverage of particular groups: persons living in collective households, armed forces, and non-resident persons working within the economic territory of the country are generally not surveyed in LFSs;
- non-coverage of certain activities: The LFS may not include hours worked in certain activities such as subsistence work and volunteer work;
- non-coverage of some territories: The LFS may not cover the entire economic territory covered in GDP.

In practice, the effective quantity of labour input depends not only on the total number of hours actually worked but also on the characteristics of those performing the work, like education, working experience, business function and sex. The measure of labour input used in this publication, i.e. total number of hours worked, does not account for the composition or heterogeneity of the labour force, thus ignoring changes in the quality of labour (i.e. human capital). This implies treating workers as perfect substitutes: an hour worked by a highly-experienced surgeon and an hour worked by an eighteen-year old student employed in a fast-food are treated as equal amounts of labour. Unadjusted measures of labour input, i.e. total number of hours worked, underestimate the effective use of labour in production affecting cross-country comparability.

Hours worked data in the *OECD Productivity Statistics* (database) (PDB)

In the *PDB*, the main requirement is that the most internationally comparable hours worked data are used (OECD, 2007). The preferred source for total hours worked is the *National Accounts* which are presented in the *OECD National Accounts Statistics* (database), both for the total economy and for aggregate economic activities. However, long time series of hours worked are not available for a number of countries; in which case, the Secretariat estimates hours worked using the *OECD Employment and Labour Market Statistics* (database), which is based on annual national LFS results supplemented with information from a detailed OECD survey sent to member countries. Total economy estimates of average hours actually worked per year and per person employed are currently available on an annual basis, for all 34 OECD member countries as follows:

- Actual hours worked are primarily sourced from the OECD *National Accounts Statistics* (database) for Australia, Austria, Belgium, Canada, the Czech Republic, Denmark, Estonia, Finland, France, Germany, Greece, Hungary, Ireland, Israel, Italy, Korea, Latvia, Lithuania, Luxembourg, Mexico, the Netherlands, Norway, Poland, Portugal, the Slovak Republic, Slovenia, South Africa, Spain, Sweden, Switzerland, the United Kingdom and the United States.
- Actual hours worked are sourced from the *OECD Employment and Labour Market Statistics* (database) for Chile, Iceland, Japan, New Zealand, the Russian Federation and Turkey.

For some countries, longer time series and/or more recent estimates of total hours worked are derived from the *OECD Economic Outlook: Statistics and Projections* (database) and national sources.

References

Ahmad, N. et al. (2003), "Comparing Labour Productivity Growth in the OECD Area: The Role of Measurement", *OECD Science, Technology and Industry Working Papers*, No. 2003/14, *http://dx.doi.org/10.1787/126534183836*.

ILO (2008), *Measurement of working time*, 18th ICLS.

OECD (2007), "Factors explaining differences in hours worked across OECD countries", *Document prepared for the Working Party No. 1 on Macroeconomic and Structural Policy Analysis*, September 2007.

OECD (2009), "Comparability of labour input measures for productivity analysis", *Document prepared for the OECD Working Party on National Accounts*, November 2009, *www.oecd.org/officialdocuments/publicdisplaydocumentpdf/?doclanguage=en&cote=std/cstat/wpna(2009)11*.

Ypma, G. and B. Van Ark (2006), "Employment and Hours Worked in National Accounts: A Producer's View on Methods and a User's View on Applicability", *EU KLEMS Working Paper* No. 10.

ANNEX C

Capital input measures at the OECD

Introduction

Two key measures of capital stock exist. The first is *productive capital stock*, which looks at capital in its function as a provider of capital services in production. The second is gross (or net) capital stock, which captures the role of capital as a store of wealth.[1] This annex provides supplementary information on these two measures, the approaches used to estimate them and capital measures available at the OECD.

Definitions

Productive capital stock (and capital services)

When the purpose of capital measurement is to gauge its role in production and productivity, via capital services, it is necessary to construct measures of the *productive capital stock*. The productive capital stock per type of capital asset is constructed by applying an age-efficiency profile and a retirement pattern when past investments of each asset are summed up over time. For example, a 10-year old lorry would be given a lower weight compared with a new lorry when past purchases of lorries are added up to construct a measure of today's productive stock of lorries. Moreover, lorries are scrapped after a certain number of years and investments that date back by say 30 years would not enter today's productive stock. Unlike gross or net capital stock measures, aggregate productive stock measures weight different types of assets by their relative productivity using the user costs of each capital type. The resulting aggregate constitutes a measure for the potential flow of productive services that all fixed assets can deliver in production.

Net and gross (wealth) capital stocks

Perhaps the best known measure of capital stock is that used to value assets on a company, industry or nation's balance sheets, that is, the gross or net capital stock measures described in the System of National Accounts (SNA). These provide measures of wealth but they are not conceptually appropriate for productivity analysis. Unlike the productive stock, the purpose of wealth capital stocks measures is not to track the role of capital as a factor of production but to track the role of capital as a set of assets with market value – wealth capital stocks appear on the balance sheets in the SNA. This reflects the fact that the implicit weighting for the different assets used in building up wealth measures of capital stock is based on the market values of the different assets. However changes in the relative productivity of the different assets are not necessarily consistent with changes in the relative price of the assets. For productivity analysis it is the former measure (and weighting of different asset types) that is relevant.

Measuring capital input

In general, capital stock series are not directly measured. In common with most measures presented in the national accounts, they are estimated by national statisticians using available underlying data with local methodology and assumptions – although there is increasing convergence towards international standards. There are heavy data requirements for the estimation of capital stocks which include the following:

- a benchmark level of capital stock for at least one year (preferably by asset type);
- a long-time-series of investment volumes and price deflators (preferably by asset type);
- as much asset type detail as possible;
- depending on the type of capital stock being estimated, estimates of average services lives by asset and/or depreciation rates for each asset;
- industry-by-asset-type investment matrices for capital stock by industry.

In this publication, capital input measures (i.e. capital services) are in line with the System of National Accounts 2008 (2008 SNA). An important recommendation of the 2008 SNA is to recognise research and development expenditure as investment (OECD, 2010). The 2008 SNA also recommends to extend the scope of fixed capital formation with the inclusion of expenditures on military equipment.

Capital measures in OECD statistics

Several OECD databases, described below, contain capital stock data. However some differences exist between them:

- *The origin of the data.* In some of the databases described below only official data made available to the OECD by national statistics institutes are used. In other databases however, particularly those that are considered more analytical databases, such as the *OECD Productivity Statistics* (database), other sources are often used to estimate missing data or to create estimates based on comparable estimation techniques.
- *The coverage of the data.* As shown in Table C.1 below, some databases are confined to aggregate statistics, such as the *OECD Economic Outlook: Statistics and Projections* (database) or *OECD Productivity Statistics* (database). Others provide a break-down by industry, such as the *OECD Structural Analysis Statistics* (database) and the OECD *National Accounts Statistics* (database).
- *The capital stock variable.* The *OECD Productivity Statistics* (database) measures productive capital stocks whereas the *OECD Structural Analysis Statistics* (database) and OECD *National Accounts Statistics* (database) contain measures of net and/or gross capital stocks.

Table C.1. **Asset and industry breakdown of capital stock data in OECD databases**

		Asset breakdown	
		Yes	No
Industry breakdown	Yes	*OECD National Accounts Statistics* (database)	*OECD Structural Analysis Statistics* (database)
	No	*OECD Productivity Statistics* (database)	*OECD Economic Outlook: Statistics and Projections* (database)

Capital services for the total economy, 8-way asset break down

Estimates of capital services in the *OECD Productivity Statistics* (database) are based on a common computation method for all countries (Schreyer et al., 2003). This approach estimates productive stock for all countries on the assumption that the same service lives are applicable for any given asset irrespective of the country.[2] The approach further uses harmonised deflators for computer hardware, telecommunications equipment and computer software and databases, for all countries, to sort out comparability problems that exist in national practices for deflation for this group of assets.

From 2015, the classification of assets adopted in the *OECD Productivity Statistics* (database) is in line with the SNA 2008 asset boundary. The flows of capital services are computed separately for eight non-residential fixed assets: computer hardware, telecommunications equipment, transport equipment, other machinery and equipment and weapons systems, non-residential construction, computer software and databases, research and development and other intellectual property products. By their very nature, capital services flows are presented as rates of change or indices and not as levels of stocks as is the case for measures of net and gross stocks.

Net and gross capital stocks by broad economic activities, with 9-way asset break-down

The *OECD National Accounts Statistics* (database) database brings together a large number of national accounts series for OECD and non-OECD countries. This includes data on net and gross capital stocks broken down by main economic activity and by nine types of assets (dwellings, other buildings and structures, transport equipment, other machinery and equipment and weapons systems, of which computer hardware and telecommunications equipment; cultivated biological resources; intellectual property products, of which computer software and databases and research and development. The data are transmitted by OECD Member countries in reply to an official questionnaire and are provided in current prices and volumes. The level of industry detail and the time period covered varies across countries.

Net and gross capital stocks by detailed industries, no asset break-down

The *OECD Structural Analysis Statistics* (database) provides data on volume measures of *gross and net capital stock* by industry. The *OECD Structural Analysis Statistics* (database) is currently moving to a new ISIC Rev.4 based industry list which covers all ISIC Rev. 4 aggregations used for national accounts, some additional 2- and 3- digit ISIC Rev. 4 detail, as well as specific aggregates. The level of industry detail and the time period covered varies across countries. A detailed overview of available data in the *OECD Structural Analysis Statistics* (database) can be found at *www.oecd.org/sti/stan*.

Alternative capital stocks, for the total economy, no asset break-down

The *OECD Economic Outlook* is a key twice-yearly publication with economic forecasts and analyses for OECD countries. One of the series available is the volume measure for non-residential capital services for the total economy (productive capital stocks).

How to access OECD capital input measures

- Aggregate capital services series in the *OECD Productivity Statistics* (database), along with methodological information and analytical papers and publications can be found on the

OECD Productivity Statistics website on *www.oecd.org/std/productivity-stats/* or on the *OECD Productivity Statistics* (database) on OECD.Stat, within the theme *Productivity*, then selecting *Growth in GDP per capita, productivity and ULC*, and then *Growth in capital input*;

- Data on gross/net capital stocks by industry can be found in the *OECD Structural Analysis Statistics* (database) on: *www.oecd.org/sti/stan*;
- Gross/net capital stocks in the *OECD National Accounts Statistics* (database) can be found under the theme of the national accounts via: *http://stats.oecd.org/*, then selecting *Annual National Accounts; Main Aggregates; Detailed Tables and Simplified Accounts; Fixed Assets by Activity and by Type of Product;*
- Data used for the *OECD Economic Outlook*, such as the total economy productive capital stock volume series, are published separately and can be found under the item *Supply Block* through the current Economic Outlook theme on OECD.Stat (*http://stats.oecd.org/*).

Notes

1. For more information on capital measures and their uses see OECD (2001, 2009) and Schreyer (2004).
2. The following average service lives are assumed for the different assets: 7 years for computer hardware, 15 years for telecommunications equipment, other machinery and equipment and weapons systems and transport equipment, 40 years for non-residential construction, 3 years for computer software and databases, 10 years for research and development and 7 years for other intellectual property products.

References

OECD (2001), *Measuring Productivity – OECD Manual: Measurement of Aggregate and Industry-Level Productivity Growth*, OECD Publishing, Paris, *http://dx.doi.org/10.1787/9789264194519-en.*

OECD (2009), *Measuring Capital – OECD Manual, Second edition*, OECD Publishing, Paris, *http://dx.doi.org/10.1787/9789264068476-en.*

OECD (2010), *OECD Handbook on Deriving Capital Measures of Intellectual Property Products*, OECD Publishing, Paris, *http://dx.doi.org/10.1787/9789264079205-en.*

Schreyer, P. (2002), "Computer Prices Indices and International Growth and Productivity Comparisons", *Review of Income and Wealth*, Number 1, Series 48.

Schreyer, P. (2004), "Capital Stocks, Capital Services and Multi-Factor Productivity Measures", *OECD Economic Studies*, Vol. 2003/2, *http://dx.doi.org/10.1787/eco_studies-v2003-art11-en.*

Schreyer, P., P. Bignon and J. Dupont (2003), "OECD Capital Services Estimates: Methodology and a First Set of Results", *OECD Statistics Working Papers*, No. 2003/06, OECD Publishing, Paris, *http://dx.doi.org/10.1787/658687860232.*

System of National Accounts (SNA) 1993, New York, *http://unstats.un.org/unsd/nationalaccount/sna1993.asp.*

System of National Accounts (SNA) 2008, New York, *http://unstats.un.org/unsd/nationalaccount/sna2008.asp.*

ANNEX D

The System of National Accounts 2008

The 2008 SNA – changes from the 1993 SNA

In 2009, The United Nations Statistical Commission endorsed a revised set of international standards for the compilation of national accounts: the System of National Accounts (SNA) 2008, replacing the 1993 version of the SNA. For Chile, China, Colombia, India, Japan, Turkey and the Russian Federation the indicators presented in this publication are in line with the 1993 SNA. For all the other countries, the indicators are based on 2008 SNA. The 2008 SNA includes a number of changes from the 1993 SNA and was adopted by most OECD countries at the end of 2014.

Changes affecting whole economy levels of income

For the United States, the adoption of the 2008 SNA in 2013 raised the level of GDP by 3.6 per cent, mainly due to the recognition of new forms of gross fixed capital formation (GFCF), notably Research and Development (R&D). The revision was also an opportunity for countries to implement some additional changes made in the 1993 SNA, which recognised entertainment originals as fixed assets. In addition changes were also made for the 2008 SNA recommendations on ownership transfer costs (see below). Current consumption expenditures of government in recent years were also revised downwards, reflecting 2008 SNA recommendations on defined benefit pensions plans as well as the net (of depreciation) effects of removing R&D expenditures from current consumption (see also below).

Research and experimental development

R&D is recognised for the first time as a produced asset. This also means that payments for the acquisition of patents, treated as acquisition or disposal of non-produced, non-financial assets in the 1993 SNA, are treated as transactions in produced assets. This also has implications for sectoral gross value added as the 2008 SNA also recommends that a separate establishment be distinguished for R&D producers when possible. See also the OECD Handbook on Deriving Capital Measures of Intellectual Property Products. Under the 1993 SNA, expenditure on R&D by government already adds to government output (which is estimated on a sum of costs basis) and subsequently as general government final consumption. So, for government the direct impact of the capitalisation mainly involves a reclassification of expenditure from government final consumption to government GFCF. Indirectly however government output and, so GDP, will increase as part of the costs of government is an imputation for depreciation; which now includes a component for the capital stock of R&D by government.

Weapons systems

Military weapons systems such as vehicles, warships, etc. used continuously in the production of defence (and deterrence) services are recognised as fixed assets in the 2008 SNA (the 1993 SNA recorded these as fixed assets only if they had dual civilian use and as intermediate consumption otherwise). Some single-use items such as certain types of ballistic missiles with a highly destructive capability, but which provide ongoing deterrence services, are also recognised as fixed assets in the 2008 SNA. Because most if not all of these expenditures are carried out by government (whose output is typically valued by summing costs) GDP will only increase by the related new consumption of fixed capital.

Financial Intermediation Services Indirectly Measured (FISIM)

The method recommended in the 2008 SNA for the calculation of FISIM implies several changes from that in the 1993 SNA. For example it explicitly recommends that FISIM only apply to loans and deposits provided by/deposited with financial institutions, and that for financial intermediaries all loans and deposits are included, not just those of intermediated funds. In addition, the 2008 SNA no longer allows countries to record FISIM as a notional industry.

Financial services

The 2008 SNA defines financial services more explicitly to ensure that services such as financial risk management and liquidity transformation, are captured.

Output of Central Banks

The 2008 SNA has provided further clarification on the calculation of FISIM in calculating the output of Centrals Banks. Where Central Banks lend or borrow at rates above or below the effective market lending/borrowing rate, the 2008 SNA recommends the recording of a tax or subsidy from the counterpart lender/borrower to/from government to reflect the difference between the two rates. Correspondingly a current transfer (the counterpart to the tax/subsidy) is recorded between government and the Central Bank. These flows will have an impact on the distribution of income in national income compared with the 1993 SNA treatment.

Output of non-life insurance services

The methodology used to indirectly estimate this activity in the 1993 SNA (premiums plus premium supplements minus claims) could lead to extremely volatile (and negative) series in cases of catastrophic losses. The 2008 SNA recommends a different indirect approach to measurement that better reflects the pricing structures used by insurance companies and the underlying provision of insurance services per se. The approach can be simply described as an ex ante expectation approach. Output is equal to premiums plus expected premium supplements minus expected claims. The 2008 SNA also recommends that exceptionally large claims, following a catastrophe, be recorded as capital, rather than current, transfers which will have an impact on (particularly sectoral) estimates of disposable income.

Valuation of output for own final use

The 2008 SNA recommends that estimates of output for own final use should include a component for the return to capital as part of the sum of costs approach when comparable market prices are not available. However no return to capital should be included for non-market producers.

Costs of ownership transfer

The 1993 SNA recommended that these costs (treated as GFCF in the accounts) should be written off over the life of the related asset. The 2008 SNA instead recommends that these costs be written off over the period the asset is expected to be held by the purchaser. This will impact on measures of net income and only marginally on gross measures, reflecting the calculation of output for own final use and government output (which is calculated as the sum of costs including depreciation).

Re-allocating income across categories

Goods sent abroad for processing

The 2008 SNA recommends that imports and exports be recorded on a strict ownership basis. This means that the values of a flow of goods moving from one country (that retains ownership of the goods) to another providing processing services should not be recorded. Only the charge for the processing service should be recorded in the trade statistics. The 1993 SNA imputed an effective change of ownership.

Merchanting

Under the 1993 SNA merchanting - the purchase and subsequent resale of goods abroad without substantial transformation and without the goods entering or exiting the territory of the merchant - was classified as a services transaction. This treatment caused global imbalances in goods and services because while the merchant records an export of a service the country acquiring the good records an import of a good. Therefore, the 2008 SNA recommends classifying merchanting as a component of trade in goods. The acquisition of goods by the merchant are recorded as negative exports of the merchant's economy and the subsequent resale of goods by the merchant are recorded as a positive exports. The difference between sales and purchases of merchanted goods is recorded under a new category "Net exports of goods under merchanting" of the merchant's economy.

Defined benefit pension schemes

The 1993 SNA stated that actual social contributions by employers and employees should reflect the amounts actually paid. The 2008 SNA differs, recognising that the amounts actually set aside may not match the liability to the employees. As such, the 2008 SNA recommends that the employer's contribution should reflect the increase in the net present value of the pension entitlement plus costs charged by the pension fund minus the employee's own contributions. This change will result in a shift of income between gross operating surplus and compensation of employees and between institutional sectors (corporations/government and households).

In some cases, a defined benefit pension plan may be underfunded implying the pension plan has insufficient financial assets to earn the returns that are necessary to meet promised future benefits. The promised future benefits are assets of the household sector and liabilities of the pension schemes, or the employer if there is no autonomous scheme. According to the 1993 SNA, only the funded component of pension plans should be reflected in liabilities. However, the new 2008 SNA recognises the importance of the liabilities of employers' pension schemes, regardless of whether they are funded or unfunded. For pensions provided by government to their employees, countries have some flexibility in the recording of the unfunded liabilities in the set of core tables. However, the full range of information is required in a new standard table (SNA Table 17.10) that shows the liabilities and associated flows of all private and public pension schemes, whether funded or unfunded, including social security.

Ancillary activities

The 2008 SNA recommends that if the activity of a unit undertaking purely ancillary activities is statistically observable (separate accounts, separate location) it should be recognised as a separate establishment.

Holding companies

The 2008 SNA recommends that holding companies should always be allocated to the financial corporations sector even if all their subsidiary corporations are non-financial corporations. The 1993 SNA recommended that they be assigned to the institutional sector in which the main group of subsidiaries was concentrated.

Exceptional payments from public corporations

The 2008 SNA recommends that these should be recorded as withdrawals from equity when made from accumulated reserves or sales of assets. The 1993 SNA treated such transactions as dividends.

Exceptional payments from governments to quasi-public corporations

The 2008 SNA recommends that these should be treated as capital transfers to cover accumulated losses and as additions to equity when a valid expectation of a return in the form of property income exists. The 1993 SNA treated all such payments as additions to equity.

References

System of National Accounts (SNA) 1993, New York, *http://unstats.un.org/unsd/nationalaccount/sna1993.asp.*

System of National Accounts (SNA) 2008, New York, *http://unstats.un.org/unsd/nationalaccount/sna2008.asp.*

Van de Ven, P. (2015), "New standards for compiling national accounts: what's the impact on GDP and other macro-economic indicators?", *OECD Statistics Brief*, No. 20, OECD Publishing, Paris, *www.oecd.org/std/na/new-standards-for-compiling-national-accounts-SNA2008-OECDSB20.pdf.*

ANNEX E

Measuring producer prices and productivity growth in services

The price index-productivity link

Empirical evidence presented in this publication points to relatively low productivity growth rates over long periods for several service industries. This is true even for some business sector services for which rapid technological change and increasing competitive pressures may argue for an opposite trend. However, for some services, this evidence may reflect an underestimation of service productivity growth, linked to difficulties measuring price indices, and hence volume series of services value added (Wölfl, 2003). While problems estimating an appropriate price index may arise in several manufacturing industries, there are reasons that measurement problems may be stronger in the service sector than in manufacturing.

Because of the difficulty in measuring services producer price indices (SPPIs), different methods are used in OECD countries to compute volume series of value added. Moreover, even if producer price indices can be computed, different methods are typically used depending on the type of the service under consideration as well as data and availability. Over the past 10 years, much progress has been made by OECD countries in measuring SPPIs, in particular in business sector services. This has significantly increased the availability of SPPIs and has improved their comparability across countries. However, even where SPPIs have been computed, they are based on different pricing methods across industries and countries, potentially affecting comparability of productivity growth estimates.

General measurement issues when tracking price changes for services

Measurement of price changes in services is not trivial, in large part complicated by the way businesses provide and charge for services, by problems identifying quality change, through the provision of bundled services, and by the difficulty identifying separate price indices per end-user.

Pricing methods

The way businesses provide and charge for services can make it difficult for statisticians to observe prices for a repeated service transaction. As such, standard price measurement methods designed for repeated products can be difficult to apply for services. In practice, price statisticians are then obliged to use a number of methods to track price changes in services, with the methods typically varying across countries, depending on the pricing mechanisms used, and also on the producing industry or product.

However, over the last 10 years, considerable efforts have been made by price statisticians to provide a better understanding of the variety of methods used by countries to facilitate international comparability and hence improve matters. The three main classes of pricing methods[1] are:

1. **Price of final service output:** Price observations refer directly to specified service outputs and result in prices of final services output; examples are: direct use of prices of repeated services, contract pricing, unit value, percentage fee, component pricing and model pricing.
2. **Time-based prices:** price observations refer to the time used for the provision of the service rather than to the service itself. Several time-based methods can be distinguished: hourly charge out rate, hourly list rate, wage rates and working days.
3. **Margin prices:** price observations refer to the price that would have to be paid by the service provider for the good or service they provided and the price paid by the final consumer.

It is important to bear in mind that how firms in a given sector charge for their products can impact considerably on the reliability of measured price indices of the index for the industry. For example, when price indices are either based on a specified service output or are time-based, results of pricing methods can have a different interpretation. In the first case, the volume of output is, in principle, correctly measured (albeit depending on how well price-determining factors are specified). However, this is not necessarily the case for time-based methods, particularly whenever quality changes have occurred, or productivity changes impact on the input (hours spent). Indeed, for pricing based on working time, the price of the service finally provided is not identified. Rather, service provision is assumed to correspond directly or predominantly to different types of chargeable hours, actually worked for a client. The validity of the method depends on how realistic this assumption is, i.e., to what extent the quantity and quality of one chargeable hour's work remains the same in consecutive periods.

Quality changes

While in principle, the same quality adjustment methods can be used for goods and services, in practice, for services, fewer options are available and much more difficult to implement (Loranger, 2012). First, over time, the way in which a certain service is provided may change (e.g. a service is delivered in less time or by a better qualified employee). Second, the structure of services that are provided in a certain service industry will vary from one period to the next. Third, many service products are unique. In this case, prices cannot be observed over multiple periods requiring assumptions about quality changes that are mostly based on convention rather than reflecting "reality"; typically, constant quality is assumed.

Treatment of bundled services

Services are frequently (and increasingly) bundled with either another service or a good. This is particularly true in the case of Transport and storage and Information and communication services. Two main alternatives are commonly used: i) breaking down the bundle into components and price these separately, or ii) pricing bundled services together as a group. Each of these alternatives poses difficulties that are likely to imply biased measure of prices. A particular concern is keeping the bundle constant over time either through quality adjustment or regular updating of the selected bundled services. The ability to reflect the non-monetary benefits of the bundle in the price index may also be a complicated task. Finally, the treatment of bundled services may lead to a heavy calculation and response burden, in particular where bundled components are priced separately.

Decomposition by type of end-users

Breaking down SPPIs by type of user is an important requirement for the national accounts when price discrimination occurs which feeds through into heterogeneous price changes. Currently, decompositions of SPPI by type of end-users focus mainly on Business to Business (BtoB), Business to Consumers (BtoC) and Business to All (BtoAll) transactions.

The potential role of price measurement for measured productivity growth

Table E.1 provides some indication of the potential effects on volume series of value added that may result from using different deflators for two services "Telecommunication services", on the one hand, and "legal and accounting services", on the other.[2] These services provide two interesting examples of how price index measurement could impact on measured productivity growth.[3] They are i) characterised by very different factors of service output and the way they are provided, and ii) by different availability of producer price indices and underlying methods.

The table provides evidence for France and the United States, for which time series data are available for a large range of input and output variables, such that several different price and volume indices can be derived. The different deflators compared are those that are commonly used in countries either directly for a deflator of value added or as a reference for the computation of producer price indices:

- *Producer Price Indices (SPPI)*. From a methodological point of view, using SPPIs, especially in the form of a *price of final service output* as defined above, would represent the most appropriate way to deflate value added if the aim is the computation of productivity growth. Ideally, SPPIs would exist for both, gross output and intermediate inputs used in producing the good or service under consideration, and SPPIs would adjust for quality changes so that the resulting value added volume series reflect productivity growth changes properly.
- *Consumer Price Indices (CPI)*, for goods or services that are close to the services analysed, or the *CPI All items*. Using CPI's for deflation may result in measurement biases vis-à-vis SPPIs as they cover only household consumption and are not valued in basic prices. This may be particularly relevant for those services where the share of final household consumption in total output is low, and where price changes differ significantly between intermediate (business) and final use (consumption) (Eurostat, 2001).
- *Wage rate indices* per employed person or per hour worked (WRIE, WRIH). The latter can be seen as a proxy for a *time-based producer price index* as defined above. Productivity growth rates based on wage rate indices may underestimate true productivity developments.

The table suggests that the choice of the implicit value added deflator, or the pricing method for computing producer price indices, may matter significantly for measured labour productivity growth. For instance, in telecommunication services, average annual labour productivity growth rates over the 2000-11 period would differ by between 5 percentage points (United States, both periods) and 10 percentage points (France, 2005-11) using different deflators. In the case of legal services, the overall variation is with 1 to 4 percentage points lower, but still significant, especially given the generally lower level of productivity growth in this services activity.

Table E.1. **Average annual growth rates in gross value added per person employed using different deflators of value added, in %**

			Base	Wage rate employment	CPI – all items	CPI – related service	SPPI
France	Telecommunications services	2000-10	6.37	0.55	2.71	6.32	
		2005-10	4.73	-2.01	0.22	4.92	8.60
	Legal and accounting services	2000-10	-0.24		1.17	1.02	
		2005-10	-1.18	-3.26	-0.88	-1.58	-2.70
United States	Broadcasting & telecommunication	2000-10	6.82	2.28	1.88	7.41	6.00
		2005-10	5.64	0.40	0.85	5.67	3.12
	Legal services	2000-10	-1.60	-0.28	0.53	-1.65	-2.68
		2005-10	-3.00	-1.13	-0.36	-1.88	-4.12

Note: All results based on double deflation. "Base": value added deflator as given in National Accounts.
Source: OECD *Structural Analysis Statistics* (database), INSEE, Bureau of Labour Statistics.

Notes

1. A pricing method is a procedure put in place by statisticians to make price data eligible to be entered in an index which is largely determined by the *pricing mechanism* (Fraisse, 2013)
2. This exercise is of a purely hypothetical nature. Its aim is to simulate how value added volume series and hence productivity growth could be affected if different pricing methods were used.
3. In the empirical results presented in Table 1, labour productivity growth has been calculated as real value added per employment and not per hour worked. While hours worked is typically the more appropriate measure of labour input, employment has been chosen here for data availability reasons.
4. The frequency of observations relative to quarterly data is 1/4 for annual data and of 3 for monthly data.

References

Fraisse, A.-S., (2013), "The new SPPI Guide, issues and challenges", *Paper presented for the Ottawa Group meeting*, Statistics Denmark, Copenhagen, May 2013.

Loranger, A. (2012), "Quality Change for Services Producer Price Indexes", *Paper presented at the Group of Experts on Consumer Price Indices*, Geneva, Switzerland, May 30-June 1 2012.

Eurostat (2001), *Handbook on price and volume measures in national accounts*, Eurostat, Luxemburg.

Wölfl, A. (2003), "Productivity Growth in Service Industries: An Empirical Assessment of Recent Patterns and the Impact of Measurement", *Science, Technology and Industry Working Paper* 2003-07, OECD Publishing, Paris, *http://dx.doi.org/10.1787/086461104618*.

ANNEX F

Purchasing power parities

Definition

Purchasing power parities (PPPs) are the rates of currency conversion that equalise the purchasing power of different currencies by eliminating the differences in price levels between countries. In their simplest form, PPPs are price relatives which show the ratio of the prices in national currencies of the same good or service in different countries. In this sense, they are spatial price comparisons.

Levels of GDP in a given year, when converted with PPPs, measure the size of economies in volume terms and so provide a more meaningful measure of the relative size of countries than simple exchange-rate based comparisons. Indeed, exchange rates reflect so many more influences than the direct price comparisons that are required to make volume comparisons. Furthermore, they tend to exhibit large movements over short periods of time, implying rapid changes in living standards which cannot have possibly occurred.

GDP and its components, converted using PPPs, provide a snapshot of relative volumes in a particular year. For many analytical purposes, the interest is in the evolution of GDP volumes between countries and over time. There are at least two ways of setting up such a comparison, each with its specific interpretation and use.

Current PPPs and expenditures (comparison at current international prices)

One approach for combining spatial and temporal observations is to use a sequence of current PPPs, i.e., a new set of price data for every period, compiled, weighted and aggregated to yield rates of currency conversion for total GDP and its expenditure components. With current PPPs, prices and price structures are allowed to vary over time. Volume levels of GDP are then obtained by applying these current PPPs, for every period, to GDP measures at current national prices. For a given year, (spatial) comparisons between countries are straightforward – volumes are measured with the same price structure. Comparisons of the resulting series over time, however, incorporate several effects: relative volume changes, changes in relative prices between countries and, possibly, changes in definitions and methodologies. The approach can also be described as comparisons at **current international prices.**

Constant PPPs and expenditures (comparison at constant international prices)

A second approach is to generate time series at constant prices and constant PPPs. With constant PPPs, a single year is chosen for the comparison of GDP levels and all other observations are obtained by applying relative rates of GDP growth, consistent with those derived in national currencies. This procedure ensures transitivity over space and time. The approach can also be described as comparisons at **constant international prices**. The key conceptual difference between using current and constant PPPs is that the former capture changes in volume as well as changes in weights, whereas the latter only capture volume changes. Put differently, even if the volumes of goods and services remain identical over time, a GDP comparison based on current PPPs may change over time if prices and price structures shift. Ignoring such shifts over longer periods can generate a biased picture of economic developments. This factor comes into play when some countries are large producers and exporters of products with marked price changes, for example Norway, which is an important oil exporter. Another consequence of fixing price structures to a base year is the sensitivity of results to the choice of the base year.

How are PPPs calculated?

PPPs are calculated in three stages:

- first for individual products,

- then for groups of products or basic headings and,

- finally, for groups of basic headings or aggregates.

The PPPs for basic headings are un-weighted averages of the PPPs for individual products. The PPPs for aggregates are weighted averages of the PPPs for basic headings.

The weights used are the expenditures on the basic headings. PPPs at all stages are price relatives. They show how many units of currency A need to be spent in country A to obtain the same volume of a product or a basic heading or an aggregate that X units of currency B purchases in country B.

In the case of a single product, the "same volume" means "identical volume". But in the case of the complex assortment of goods and services that make up an aggregate such as GDP, the "same volume" does not mean an "identical basket of goods and services".

The composition of the basket will vary between countries according to their economic, social and cultural differences, but each basket will provide equivalent satisfaction or utility.

- Values at constant international prices of period t_0 (at PPPs of period t_0)

Values at constant international prices of period t_0 (at PPPs of period t_0) are series at current domestic prices converted to a common currency by way of constant PPPs of a given year.

Constant PPPs capture volume changes only.

A value index of this kind corresponds to a weighted average of the value changes in domestic prices, as PPPs are held fixed.

- Values at constant international prices of period t_{-1} (at PPPs of period t_{-1})

Values at constant international prices of period t_{-1} (at PPPs of period t_{-1}) are series at current domestic prices converted to a common currency by way of PPPs of year t_{-1}.

A value index of this kind corresponds to a weighted average of the value changes in domestic prices, as PPPs are held fixed at their previous year's value. However, weights are continuously updated.

- Values at current international prices (at current PPPs)

Values at current international prices (at current PPPs) are series at current domestic prices converted to a common currency by way of current PPPs. Because PPPs are price relatives of goods and services, this implies substituting the set of domestic prices by a set of international prices.

Current PPPs capture changes in volumes and in relative prices.

References

Bournot S., F. Koechlin and P. Schreyer (2011), "2008 Benchmark PPPs Measurement and Uses", *OECD Statistics Brief*, No. 17, OECD Publishing, Paris, *www.oecd.org/std/47359870.pdf*.

Schreyer P. and F. Koechlin (2002), "Purchasing power parities – measurement and uses", *OECD Statistics Brief*, No. 3, OECD Publishing, Paris, *www.oecd.org/std/prices-ppp/2078177.pdf*.

OECD/Eurostat (2012), *Eurostat-OECD Methodological Manual on Purchasing Power Parities (2012 Edition)*, OECD Publishing, Paris, *http://dx.doi.org/10.1787/9789264189232-en*.

OECD (2008), *OECD Glossary of Statistical Terms*, OECD Publishing, Paris, *http://dx.doi.org/10.1787/9789264055087-en*.

OECD, *Purchasing Power Parities* (PPP), *www.oecd.org/std/prices-ppp/*.

ANNEX G

Trends

Understanding to which extent productivity growth is driven by structural factors and affected by short-term economic fluctuations is of utmost importance for policy makers. To shed light on this distinction, one can decompose the series into a trend and a cyclical component, where the trend is meant to capture the long-term growth of the series and the cyclical component is the deviation of the series from that trend. In the OECD Compendium of Productivity Indicators 2015, the method used to extract the trend component is the Hodrick-Prescott (HP) filter (Hodrick and Prescott, 1997).

The Hodrick-Prescott filter

The HP filter is the best known and most widely used method to separate the trend from the cycle (Hodrick and Prescott, 1997). The method has been first presented in a working paper in 1981 (Hodrick and Prescott, 1981). The filter is defined as the solution to the following optimisation problem:

$$y_t = \tau_t + c_t$$

$$min_{\{\tau_t\}}\left\{\sum_{t=1}^{T}(y_t-\tau_t)^2+\lambda\sum_{t=2}^{T-1}\left[(\tau_{t+1}-\tau_t)-(\tau_t-\tau_{t-1})\right]^2\right\}$$

where y_t is the original series, τ_t is the trend component and c_t is the cyclical component. The method consists of minimising the deviation of the original series from the trend (the first term of the equation) as well as the curvature of the estimated trend (the second term). The trade-off between the two goals is governed by the smoothing parameter λ. The higher the value of λ, the smoother is the estimated trend.

For quarterly data it has been typically assumed a value of $\lambda = 1600$, as recommended by Hodrick and Prescott (1997). However, there is less agreement on the value to be used when the filter is applied to other frequencies (e.g. annual, monthly). Backus and Kehoe (1992) used $\lambda = 100$ for annual data, while Ravn and Uhlig (2002) propose an adjustment of the standard value of 1600 that consists of multiplying that value by the fourth power of the frequency of observations relative to quarterly data. The latter results in a value of λ equal to 6.25 ($1600^*(1/4)^4$) for annual data.[4]

The HP-filter can be interpreted in the frequency domain. In this formulation the λ parameter can be associated with the cut-off frequency of the filter – the frequency at which it halves the impact of the original cyclical component. It can be shown that the Ravn-Uhlig rule for selecting the value of λ corresponds to a cut-off frequency of approximately 10 years, assuming annual data (Maravall and Del Río 2001). Nonetheless, Nilsson and Gyomai (2011) point out that the HP-filter has strong leakages (i.e. letting cyclical components from the stop band appear in the filtered series), and this feature may affect the choice of the filter parameter depending on the goal of the study and sensitivity to filter leakage.

In this publication, the target frequency for trend estimation was no different than in the above studies (10 years and beyond). However an additional objective is to minimize the leakage from shorter business-cycle frequencies into the estimated trend. Accordingly, the value of the smoothing parameter selected here is $\lambda = 54.12$. This value has been determined by calibrating the Hodrick-Prescott filter in such a way that the frequency response at 9.5 years is equal to 0.10. This means that with $\lambda = 54.12$, cycles with a wavelength lower than 9.5 years would be attenuated by 90% or more.

In comparison with other *ideal* filters, the trend estimated with the HP filter is more sensitive to transitory shocks or short-term fluctuations at the end of the sample period. This results in a sub-optimal performance of the HP filter at the endpoints of the series (Baxter and King, 1999). In view of this property, in order to lessen revisions of the published estimates, trend series are not published for the last two years for which data on the original series are available. Even though, the choice of the HP filter is based on its interpretability and widespread use in the literature.

References

Backus D. and P. Kehoe (1992), "International evidence on the historical properties of business cycles", *The American Economic Review*, Vol. 82, No. 4.

Hodrick R. and E. Prescott (1981), "Postwar U.S. business cycles: an empirical investigation", Carnegie Mellon University, *Discussion paper* No. 451.

Hodrick R. and E. Prescott (1997), "Postwar U.S. business cycles: an empirical investigation", *Journal of Money, Credit and Banking*, Vol. 29, No. 1.

Maraval, A. and A. Del Río (2001), "Time aggregation and the Hodrick-Prescott filter", Banco de España, Servicios de Estudios, *Documento the trabajo* No. 0108.

Nilsson, R. and G. Gyomai (2011), "Cycle Extraction: A Comparison of the Phase-Average Trend Method, the Hodrick-Prescott and Christiano-Fitzgerald Filters", *OECD Statistics Working Papers*, No. 2011/04, OECD Publishing, Paris, *http://dx.doi.org/10.1787/5kg9srt7f8g0-en*.

Ravn M. and H. Uhlig (2002), "On adjusting the Hodrick-Prescott filter for the frequency of observations", *The Review of Economics and Statistics*, Vol. 84, No. 2.

ORGANISATION FOR ECONOMIC CO-OPERATION AND DEVELOPMENT

The OECD is a unique forum where governments work together to address the economic, social and environmental challenges of globalisation. The OECD is also at the forefront of efforts to understand and to help governments respond to new developments and concerns, such as corporate governance, the information economy and the challenges of an ageing population. The Organisation provides a setting where governments can compare policy experiences, seek answers to common problems, identify good practice and work to co-ordinate domestic and international policies.

The OECD member countries are: Australia, Austria, Belgium, Canada, Chile, the Czech Republic, Denmark, Estonia, Finland, France, Germany, Greece, Hungary, Iceland, Ireland, Israel, Italy, Japan, Korea, Luxembourg, Mexico, the Netherlands, New Zealand, Norway, Poland, Portugal, the Slovak Republic, Slovenia, Spain, Sweden, Switzerland, Turkey, the United Kingdom and the United States. The European Commission takes part in the work of the OECD.

OECD Publishing disseminates widely the results of the Organisation's statistics gathering and research on economic, social and environmental issues, as well as the conventions, guidelines and standards agreed by its members.

OECD PUBLISHING, 2, rue André-Pascal, 75775 PARIS CEDEX 16
(30 2016 01 1 P) ISBN 978-92-64-25019-2 – 2016

www.ingramcontent.com/pod-product-compliance
Lightning Source LLC
Chambersburg PA
CBHW061221240926
51846CB00006B/1302
* 9 7 8 9 2 6 4 2 5 0 1 8 5 *